Remembering Anna O.

Remembering Anna O.

A Century of Mystification

Mikkel Borch-Jacobsen

Translated by Kirby Olson
in collaboration with Xavier Callahan and the author

Routledge
New York and London

Published in 1996 by
Routledge
29 West 35th Street
New York, NY 10001

Published in Great Britain by
Routledge
11 New Fetter Lane
London EC4P 4EE

Library of Congress Cataloging-in-Publication Data

Borch-Jacobsen, Mikkel.
    [Souvenirs d'Anna O. English]
    Remembering Anna O. : a century of mystification /
    Mikkel Borch-Jacobsen: translated by Kirby Olson
    in collaboration with Xavier Callahan and the author.
    p.   cm.
    ISBN 0-415-91776-X (alk. paper)
    1. Psychoanalysis—History. I. Title.
    BF173.B684   1996
    150.19'52—dc20   96-21013
                                                CIP

I did not question her at all, for fear that any questions of mine might suggest ideas to her that were not her own. One cannot be too careful: a magnetist, when it comes to questions of this kind, often ends up directing the patient, whom he then regards as an oracle, whereas she is merely his own echo.

—Tardy de Montravel,
Journal of the Magnetic Treatment of Miss N.
(London, 1785)

Contents

Acknowledgments

This is a history book (not to mention a storybook) about psychoanalysis, by a newcomer to the field. If history is always written by many people, that is more than ordinarily true in this case. Without the help of a group of friends, all of them seasoned Freud scholars, I could never have found my way through the labyrinth of archives, purloined letters, gossip, and rumor known as Freud studies.

To Sonu Shamdasani, consummate insider, I owe my introduction to this strange and fascinating world (fascinating in the way that espionage or theology can be). The suggestions and advice that he tirelessly proffered in the course of our interminable Internet conversations are too numerous to count. Suffice it to say that this book is in his debt for what has been most essential to it: my desire to write it, and my pleasure in having done so.

The same goes for Peter Swales, who made his time

and his vast knowledge of Freudian matters completely available to me, with a generosity bordering on the reckless. I thank him warmly for giving me access both to his personal archives (which for many of us have become an alternative to the Kafkaesque Sigmund Freud Archives) and to his unpublished lecture "Freud, Breuer, and the Blessed Virgin." My own work owes a great deal to a reading of this remarkable lecture, as well as to the countless remarks and corrections that its author lavished on me while I was writing this book (saving me from, among other things, two egregious factual errors). This is the place to call attention to the extent of the unacknowledged influence that Peter Swales's *unpublished* research has had on Freud studies over the last fifteen years, and to urge that he now let his work become known beyond the circle of his friends and colleagues.

Richard Skues has my deep thanks for sharing his valuable archives with me and for conducting some research on my behalf in London, about a manuscript by Marie Bonaparte. The hints he gave me have been extremely helpful, as were those offered by Paul Roazen.

I thank Pearl King, honorary archivist of the Institute of Psycho-Analysis in London, for kindly granting access to the correspondence of Ernest Jones. My thanks go also to Marie Kann, Josef Breuer's granddaughter, for permission to reproduce a letter from her mother to Ernest Jones. Thanks as well to Elisabeth Roudinesco for carrying out some research for me in her personal archives and for allowing me to reproduce a passage from the personal journal of Marie Bonaparte, which she has in her possession. I am also most grateful to Albrecht Hirsch-müller, Lucy Freeman, and Daniel Goleman for taking the time to respond to my requests for information. My gratitude extends to Dr. Frank Hartman, too, for granting me no fewer than three telephone interviews.

I owe a great debt of thanks to my father, Niels Borch-Jacobsen, for bringing Uffe Hansen's book on Carl Hansen to my attention, a book that provided a crucial link in my argument.

This book's first, rough English translation was made possible in large part by the generous support of the Graduate School of the University of Washington. Kirby Olson and I also warmly thank Xavier Callahan for her thoroughgoing and inspired revisions of the translation, which dramatically changed it from its first rehash.

Paul Antze, having invited me to participate in a May 1994 panel discussion ("Life Stories: Trauma, Memory, and the Politics of Identity") at the annual meeting of the Canadian Anthropology Society, is responsible for prompting me to draw up the preliminary outline for this book. Where the book's final content is concerned, however, I am afraid the responsibility rests with me alone.

CHAPTER ONE

Our Myth

Every society has its therapeutic myths, meant to explain why we fall ill and why we get well, and our society is no exception. To be sure, we no longer imagine that our ills are caused by spirits or evil omens, nor do we believe any longer in curative powers derived from the laying on of hands or from magical formulas. But we are quick to believe that certain troubles, which we call *psychological* or *psychosomatic*, are due to traumatic events in our personal histories, and that by recounting these events to a doctor we will cure ourselves of their effects. It is necessary, we believe, to name the ill, narrate it, *make the evil speak*, in order to be rid of it. This idea is hardly new. Far from it: it stems from the Christian practices of confession and exorcism, by way of the Protestant "cure of the soul." But with the "medicalization of confession" set in motion by Freud, it became one of the most widely accepted notions of our psychoanalytic century, now drawing to a close.[1] Who has any doubt nowadays that our past is the key to our present, and that by articulating this past, verbalizing it to a therapist, we can divest ourselves of its debilitating weight? Memory liberates, narration heals, history redeems: this idea seems to us so constitutive of what we call *psychotherapy* (in the widest sense) that we have forgotten what Freud's immediate precursors understood by this word—namely, a therapy based on the "suggestive" speech *of the doctor*, and not at all on the speech of the patient.[2] So natural does this idea seem to us that we freely apply it to the therapeutic myths of other societies, viewing those myths as primitive or crude forms of psychotherapy, never stopping to wonder what makes our native theory so superior to theirs.

But why, after all, must I recount my life story instead of having a shaman pull some object out of my body? Why are my demons necessarily memories or inner obsessions instead of external spiritual entitites?[3] Why should the cause of my symptoms be sought in the past instead of in a curse put on me by some rival? And why in

1. Michel Foucault, *La Volonté de savoir* (Paris: Gallimard, 1976), p. 90.
2. Daniel Hack Tuke, *Illustrations of the Influence of the Mind upon the Body in Health and Disease designed to elucidate the Action of the Imagination* (London: J. & A. Churchill, 1872) (see especially the chapter titled "Psycho-therapeutics—Practical Applications of the Influence of the Mind on the Body to Medical Practice"); Hippolyte Bernheim, *Hypnotisme, suggestion, psychothérapie. Etudes nouvelles* (Paris: Doin, 1891); Sigmund Freud, "Psychical (or Mental) Treatment" (1890), in *The Standard Edition of the Complete Psychological Works of Sigmund Freud*, ed. by J. Strachey, 24 vols. (London: The Hogarth Press, 1953–74), VII, pp. 281–302 (*Standard Edition* hereafter abbreviated *SE*).
3. "The split-off mind is the devil with which the unsophisticated observation of early superstitious times believed that these patients were

my past instead of in my family's or my clan's, or in some
mythical lineage? The fact is, we rarely bother to ask such
questions. And even when we do, we usually respond,
just like other native informants, with stories that supposedly justify our systematized beliefs. The details of
these stories may vary endlessly, but the *ur*-pattern is
always the same: "One day, X said *y* to Z, and, lo and
behold, his symptom disappeared for good." Here, we
recognize the story that Josef Breuer told about the spectacular cure of Fräulein Anna O., his patient: "It was in
the summer during a period of extreme heat, and the
patient was suffering very badly from thirst; for, without
being able to account for it in any way, she suddenly
found it impossible to drink. She would take up the glass
of water she longed for, but as soon as it touched her lips
she would push it away like someone suffering from
hydrophobia. [. . .] This had lasted for some six weeks,
when one day during hypnosis she grumbled about her
English lady-companion whom she did not care for, and
went on to describe, with every sign of disgust, how she
had once gone into that lady's room and how her little
dog—horrid creature!—had drunk out of a glass there.
The patient had said nothing, as she wanted to be polite.
After giving further energetic expression to the anger she
had held back, she asked for something to drink, drank a

---

possessed. It is true that a spirit alien to the patient's waking consciousness holds sway in him; but the spirit is not in fact an alien one, but a
part of his own" (Josef Breuer, "Theoretical," in Josef Breuer and Sigmund Freud, *Studies on Hysteria* [1895], *SE* II, p. 250; *Studies on Hysteria* hereafter abbreviated *SH*).

large quantity of water without any difficulty and woke from her hypnosis with the glass at her lips; and thereupon the disturbance vanished, never to return."[4]

This, to be sure, is still a far cry from the tales of childhood "seduction" that Freud would obtain from his patients between 1896 and 1897, and farther yet from the sensational accounts of incest and satanic ritual abuse that have become all the rage lately among American therapists. Right here, however, in this rather innocuous account of Anna O., is where the idea was born that "hysterics suffer mainly from reminiscences,"[5] as Breuer and Freud state in *Studies on Hysteria*, and that these traumatic memories can be "talked away"[6] under hypnosis. Of course, this sturdy theory soon underwent a number of metamorphoses: Freud reconceptualized Breuer's indeterminate "trauma," first as an actual sexual assault suffered in early childhood, then as a fantasy having to do with perverse infantile sexuality, and finally as a fantasy of Oedipal origin. As for cathartic hypnosis, it was abandoned in favor of the method of so-called free association, which itself gradually came to be recentered on the analysis of resistances and of the transference. But none of these reshufflings ever called the fundamental, seminal idea into question: that *to remember is to heal*. Heal from what? From the amnesia that "dissociates" the psyche, from the forgetting that breaks the continuity of my history and

---

4. J. Breuer, "Fräulein Anna O.," in *SH*, pp 34–35.
5. J. Breuer and S. Freud, "On the Psychological Mechanism of Hysterical Phenomena: Preliminary Communication," *SH*, p. 7.
6. *SH*, p. 35.

therefore keeps me from being my *self*. Ever since (and because of) Anna O.'s miraculous cure, forgetting has ceased to be a simple lapse of memory and has become, under various names—"dissociated consciousness," "the unconscious," "repression"—the supreme form of remembering, and the very key to our identity as subjects.

Freud himself said this quite overtly in 1917: "This discovery of Breuer's is still the foundation of psychoanalytic therapy. The thesis that symptoms disappear when we have made their unconscious predeterminants conscious has been confirmed by all subsequent research, although we meet with the strangest and most unexpected complications when we attempt to carry it through in practice."[7] Are we much more advanced now that a hundred years have gone by since the publication of *Studies on Hysteria*? Apparently not, to judge by the spectacular comeback, in the United States, of the traumatic-dissociative etiology of neurosis, with its parade of "traumatic memories" abreacted under hypnosis. And even if the theorists of "recovered memory" do refer to Janet more than to Breuer or Freud, it is clear that their utter trust in remembering, with its "integrative" power, takes us more directly back to Anna O.'s "talking cure" than to the suggestive manipulation of memories practiced by the

---

7. S. Freud, *Introductory Lectures on Psychoanalysis* (1916–1917), *SE* XV–XVI, p. 280.

8. On this point, see the excellent article by Ruth Leys, "Traumatic Cures: Shell Shock, Janet, and the Question of Memory," *Critical Inquiry* 20 (Summer 1994). Ruth Leys correctly points out that the famous cure of Marie, described by Janet in *Psychological Automatisim*, rested not on remembering but on *removal of* the pathogenic memory.

author of *Psychological Automatism*.[8] Consider this description of "trauma work" in Judith Herman's recent book: "In the second stage of recovery, the survivor tells the story of the trauma. [...] This work of reconstruction actually transforms the traumatic memory, so that it can be integrated into the survivor's life story. [...] Out of the fragmented components of frozen imagery and sensation, patient and therapist slowly reassemble an organized, detailed, verbal account, oriented in time and historical context. [...] The ultimate goal [...] is to put the story, including its imagery, into words."[9]

Are things very different at the other end of the Freudian spectrum, among the Lacanians and the American narrativists (such as Roy Schafer and Donald Spence)? Aware of the reconstructive and "hermeneutic" character of memory (and taking a lesson from Freud's difficulties in this area), they no longer believe in the "historical truth" of memories obtained on the analytic couch. Lacan, referring directly to the "talking cure" of Anna O. and to "the discovery of the pathogenic event dubbed the traumatic experience," said this as long ago as

---

9. Judith Lewis Herman, *Trauma and Recovery* (New York: Basic Books, 1992), pp. 175, 177 (cited as well by Ruth Leys; see previous note). Joost Vijselaar and Onno van der Hart, two other "trauma work" theorists, write, "Among other things, hypnosis enables patients to move from experiential recall of the traumatic event (symbolically expressed in the symptoms) to conscious recollections. [...] [P]atients are thus able to put the narrative of their traumatic loss in its place as one of the chapters in their personal history" (Joost Vijselaar and Onno van der Hart, "The First Report of Hypnotic Treatment of Traumatic Grief: A Brief Communication," *International Journal of Clinical and Experimental Hypnosis* 40 [1992], 1, pp. 3–4).

1953: "If this event was recognized as being the cause of the symptom, it was because the putting into words of the event (in the patient's 'stories') determined the lifting of the symptom. [...] The fact remains that in the hypnotic state verbalization is dissociated from *prise de conscience* [awareness], and this fact alone is enough to require a revision of the conception of its effects. But why is it that the doughty advocates of the behaviorist *Aufhebung* do not use this as their example to show that they do not have to know whether the subject has remembered anything whatever from the past? He has simply recounted the event. But I would say that he has verbalized it, [...] that he has made it pass into the *verbe*, or, more precisely, into the *epos* by which he brings back into present time the origins of his person. [...] I might as well be categorical: in psychoanalytic anamnesis, it is not a question of reality, but of truth, because the effect of full speech is to reorder past contingencies by conferring on them the necessities to come."[10]

In other words, what matters is not the factual (reproductive, constative) accuracy of the memory but only the narrative (productive, performative) truth of the story through which the subject *constructs* his or her history, for the benefit of the analyst. As Donald Spence puts it, "The truth [of the narrative] lies more in the present and future than in the past. We are primarily

---

10. Jacques Lacan, "Function and Field of Speech and Language," *Ecrits: A Selection*, translated by Alan Sheridan (New York: Norton, 1977), pp. 46–48.

interested in the effect it produces rather than in its past credentials. [...] Associations and interpretations, as they are inserted into the developing narrative, become true as they become familiar and lend meaning to otherwise disconnected pieces of the patient's life. The very process that allows the analysts to understand the disconnected pieces of the hour, when extended and amplified, enables the patient to gradually see his life as continuous, coherent and therefore meaningful."[11]

The fact remains that Lacan, like his contemporary narrativist counterparts, continues to make "the completeness of the cure,"[12] as he called it in 1953, dependent on *narrative* speech—that is, on the production, whether we like it or not, of a history and a memory. For Lacan and the narrativists, anamnesis and remembering are still the foundation and the "source of therapeutic progress,"[13] even if these are conceived of as dialectical or "intersubjective" reconstruction and not simply as the photographic reproduction of trauma: "What we teach the subject to recognize as his unconscious is his history—that is to say, we help him to perfect the present historicization of the facts that have already determined a certain number of the historical 'turning points' of his existence."[14] And again: "It is certainly this assumption of his history by the subject, in so far as it is constituted by

---

11. Donald Spence, *Narrative Truth and Historical Truth* (New York: Norton, 1982), pp. 276, 280.
12. J. Lacan, *Ecrits: A Selection*, p. 47.
13. *Ibid.*, p. 46.
14. *Ibid.*, p. 52.

the speech addressed to the other, that constitutes the ground of the new method that Freud called psycho-analysis [. . .] in 1895."[15]

Myths are notoriously thick-skinned, and here we have a fine example. It may be true that the cure of Anna O. consisted—*partly*—in her relating "memories" to Breuer, but it is just plain untrue that this treatment ever got rid of her symptoms. This fact became well known in 1953, when Ernest Jones revealed it publicly in the first volume of his biography of Freud,[16] and it has since been amply corroborated by the painstaking research of Henri Ellenberger, Albrecht Hirschmüller, Ellen Jensen, and Peter Swales, among many others.[17] No one today can

15. *Ibid.*, p. 48. Lacan, who made cruel fun of a colleague for dating the first mention of psychoanalysis from 1904, is himself just as wrong to date it from 1895. Freud actually introduced the term in 1896, in his "Further Remarks on the Neuro-Psychoses of Defense." But at least this paramnesia has the virtue of showing that psychoanalysis, for Lacan, was born with *Studies on Hysteria* (1895).

16. Ernest Jones, *The Life and Work of Sigmund Freud*, vol. 1 (New York: Basic Books, 1953), pp. 223–226. We may very well ask why Lacan saw no need to modify his version of the Anna O. episode, since he had ample opportunity to read Jones's biography between the first version of "Function and Field . . . ," delivered as a lecture in September 1953, and the second version, published in the first issue of *La Psychanalyse* in 1956, to say nothing of the no less thoroughly revised third version, published in *Ecrits* in 1966.

17. Henry F. Ellenberger, "The Story of Anna O.: A Critical Review with New Data," *Journal of the History of the Behavioral Sciences* 8 (1972), pp. 267–79; Albrecht Hirschmüller, *The Life and Work of Josef Breuer. Physiology and Psychoanalysis* (New York: New York University Press, 1989) (hereafter abbreviated *JB*); Ellen M. Jensen, *Streifzüge durch das Leben von Anna O./Bertha Pappenheim. Ein Fall für die Psychiatrie—Ein Leben für die Philanthropie* (Frankfurt am Main: ZTV, 1984); Peter J. Swales, "Anna O. in Ischl," *Werkblatt* 5 (1988), pp. 57–64; "Freud, Breuer, and the Blessed Virgin," unpublished lecture delivered at New York Hospital, Cornell Medical Center (January 1986).

remain unaware that the treatment of Anna O. (whose real name was Bertha Pappenheim) was very different from what Breuer and Freud have told us about it—so different, in fact, that we can legitimately wonder what remains of modern psychotherapy's origin-myth, now that the historians of psychoanalysis have so thoroughly debunked it. But that hasn't prevented this myth and its derivatives from perpetuating themselves and proliferating in psychotherapeutic discourse (and beyond—in the culture, in our relationship to the past and to history, in the way we react to the "traumatic" events that occur in our lives). Paradoxically enough, the very myth that forms the basis of our modern belief in the redemptive value of recollection and narration has stubbornly resisted historicization. Everyone knows perfectly well that the cure of Anna O. *is* a myth, and yet everyone hastens to forget this when the theoretical, practical, institutional, and medical-legal consequences come into play (just ask the hundreds of American parents whose "adult children," accusing them of incest, are hauling them into court on the strength of "memories" dug up during psychotherapy).

Myths, as we know, are impervious to history, for the means of their validation has nothing to do with historical critique. They need no authentication by documents or witnesses; it is enough that, like rumors, they be repeated, replicated, re-cited. It was no accident that Freud talked about the great founding case histories of psychoanalysis in terms of a paradigm (*Paradigma*), a model

(*Vorbild*), and even a pattern (*Muster*).[18] These case histories are not so much faithful accounts of treatment (impossible to verify in any case, since theoretically they would be protected under medical confidentiality) as models to be imitated, and no less by psychoanalysts than by their patients. In other words, the case histories have no scientific or historical function; their function is one of identification and emulation, with every new version retroactively confirming and justifying the model. Any possibility of validation or experimental control is excluded on principle, so it goes without saying that the model can be validated only by its own replication. This is true of all Freud's great paradigmatic cases, but especially of the *ur*-paradigm that is the case of Anna O. After all, wasn't it the imitation, by Freud and his patients, of Bertha Pappenheim's treatment that retroactively "proved" the validity of her cure and convinced Breuer to publish her case history?[19] Like any other origin-myth, the

---

18. On this notion of paradigmatic cases, see Anthony Stadlen, "Dora's Illness: A Case for Historical Detection," *The Times Higher Education Supplement*, June 14, 1985.

19. As Peter Swales has pointed out, there is good reason to suspect that Anna von Lieben, the "Cäcilie M." of the *Studies on Hysteria* and one of the very first patients with whom Freud used the "cathartic method," had heard about Bertha Pappenheim's treatment, if not directly from Breuer (who had both women in treatment) then at least through the intermediary of his uncle, Theodor Gomperz, and the uncle's wife, Elise, herself a patient of Freud (Peter J. Swales, "Freud, His Teacher and the Birth of Psychoanalysis," in Paul E. Stepansky, ed., *Freud: Appraisals and Reappraisals* [New York: The Analytic Press, 1986], vol. 1, p. 41). On that score, we should note that Anna von Lieben's symptoms included a facial neuralgia, losses of sensation, and even a temporary inability to

ur-paradigm exists outside time, outside memory, outside history, because it never existed at all before its replication. We already had the Imitation of Christ, and the history of psychoanalysis has given us the Imitation of Anna O.

But, the defenders of the faith will say, why trouble ourselves about the true story of Bertha Pappenheim when the process of emulation that gave rise to psycho-analysis was set in motion by the story of Anna O.? This wily argument, so often invoked in our own day by the defenders of psychoanalysis, amounts to nothing more and nothing less than a demand for us to join the flock of the faithful and become narrators ourselves, retellers of the myth: "myth here does not mean, as it so often does when 'history' and 'myth' are contrasted, an illusion, a self-serving mask of a deliberately hidden truth. Rather myth here signifies the structure which permits the story of the origin, the birth of psychoanalysis, to be told."[20]

---

speak German, exactly as in Bertha Pappenheim's case (*ibid.*, pp. 29–30 and 71, n. 50). The recent interest in the role played by certain *ur*-patients in the elaboration of modern psychotherapeutic theories (an interest advanced by Henri Ellenberger, "La Psychiatrie et son histoire incon-nue," *L'Union médicale du Canada* 90 [March 1961]) should not cause us to forget that these patients also belonged to patient *pools*, with all the effects of interaction, feedback, and amplification that this situation implies.

20. See Lisa Appignanesi and John Forrester, *Freud's Women* (New York: Basic Books, 1992), p. 73. Elisabeth Roudinesco makes the same argument: "In this story [of Anna O.], we cannot accuse Jones of falsification. He invents a fiction, but this invention bears witness to a historical reality to which we cannot oppose the simplistic argument of a 'reality' of facts. [. . .] The truth of this story lies in [. . .] its legend and refers to the way in which the psychoanalytic movement tells itself the initial fan-tasies about its birth" (Elisabeth Roudinesco, *Histoire de la psychanalyse en France* [Paris: Le Seuil, 1986], vol. 1, p. 31).

There is no better way to say that nothing matters so much to the true believer as the re-citation of the myth. But we must also note how important it is that the myth be *original, foundational*: God (and Freud) forbid that the story of Anna O. should itself be the imitation of some other story! Mythical re-citation partakes of amnesia because it requires an absolute beginning, an absolute birth preceded by nothing. And so there are worse ways to offend the narrator than by pointing out the mythical nature of his origin-myth, since deep down he already knows all about that (the true believers are no less cynical than the priests). The real crime of lese-myth consists in demonstrating that the narration of this particular myth repeats other myths, which in turn repeat others. Let us narrate.

CHAPTER TWO

The 1895 Case History

Let us consider the case history published by Breuer in 1895—that is, thirteen years after Bertha Pappenheim's treatment ended (a delay quite interesting in its own right). The account is easy to summarize, since according to Breuer the patient's illness passed through four clearly demarcated phases:

1. A period of "latent incubation" (note the expression), extending from mid-July 1880, when the patient's father fell gravely ill with pleurisy, to December 10 of the same year. The patient was subject to "absences," hallucinations, and contractures (lasting muscular spasms) that went unnoticed by anyone around her. Anemia, anorexia, coughing fits.

2. The period of "manifest illness" (here, too, the expression should be noted) from December 11, 1880,

to April 1, 1881, with the patient staying in bed. This period was marked by the appearance of an impressive array of symptoms, "in rapid succession":[1] left-side occipital headaches; a convergent squint; disturbances of vision; paresis (mild paralysis) of the frontal muscles of the neck; various contractures; anesthesia (localized loss of sensation); hallucinations (the patient saw black snakes); fear that the walls would cave in; disturbances of speech (the patient lost her ability to speak, then seemed to be suffering from aphasia, was no longer able to speak German, and mixed up four or five foreign languages before finally settling exclusively on English, in March 1881); splitting of the personality, with the patient alternating between her normal, depressed self and a *condition seconde*[2] in which she behaved capriciously, and which she was unable to remember afterward. These trancelike states, which the patient (in English) called "clouds," and which Breuer (in French) called "*absences*" or, again, "somnambulism" or "hypnosis," were a regular feature of her late

---

1. *SH*, p. 23.
2. Breuer borrows this term from the famous case of "Félida X.," described by Eugène Azam in *Hypnotisme, double conscience et altérations de la personnalité* (Paris: Baillière, 1887). Félida, who quickly became a classic figure of split personality and "maladies of memory," alternated between a *condition prime*, in which she was serious and sad, and a *condition seconde*, in which she was frivolous and playful (this pattern was common in nineteenth-century "dual personalities," from Mary Reynolds to Miss Beauchamp). The *condition seconde* afforded recollection of the *condition prime*, but the reverse was not true (in this connection, Azam spoke of "periodic amnesia").

afternoons. Breuer notes that he was then able to calm her by having her tell sad stories "in the style of Hans Christian Andersen's *Picture-Book Without Pictures*"[3]—a procedure that the patient called (in English) the "talking cure" or "chimney sweeping." Partial remission of symptoms at the end of this period. The patient left her bed on April 1 (!), 1881.

3. A period in which the symptoms returned, extending from just after the death of the patient's father on April 5, 1881, to the beginning of December 1881. The patient refused to feed herself, had positive and negative hallucinations, and no longer recognized anyone but Breuer. She told no more charming little fairy tales in the style of Andersen, but relived and "tragedized" ("*sie durchlebend* [...] *tragierte*")[4] her morbid hallucinations. Her state worsened, and Breuer, against her will, confined her to a sanatorium from June 7, 1881, until the following autumn. When Breuer resumed treating the patient, after his summer vacation, her hydrophobia disappeared, which gave him the idea of attempting to eliminate her symptoms systematically, by having her talk about their origins while in a state of self-hypnosis.

---

3. *SH*, p. 29,
4. This reference, in Breuer's original text, to tragedy—important, since it underscores the theatricality (or histrionics) of the first "cathartic" cure—is lost in the English translation: "she acted these things through as though she was experiencing them" (*SH*, p. 27).

4.   A period extending from the beginning of December 1881 to June 7, 1882, and characterized by systematization of the treatment and/or of the illness. The patient, content until now to alternate between her "real self" and her "evil self,"[5] began to alternate between her *present* self and her *past* self. In her *condition seconde* she relived the events of the corresponding day from the year before (that is, the events from the period between the beginning of the "manifest illness," on December 11, 1880, through June 7, 1881). The startling accuracy of these relived experiences was confirmed, Breuer tells us, by the diary of the patient's mother. During the patient's evening sessions of self-hypnosis, Breuer now faced three tasks: first, to eliminate by verbal means the hallucinations and imaginative productions of the day; second, to reproduce the events of the corresponding day from the preceding year; and, third, to recapitulate one by one, "in reverse order, starting before the time when the patient became bed-ridden,"[6] every occurrence of the various symptoms that had appeared before the "incubation period" (for example, no fewer than 303 instances of hysterical deafness). To speed up this last part of the treatment (the patient resisted all his attempts to go directly to the initial trauma), Breuer hypnotized her every morning, hoping to

---

5.   *SH*, p. 24.
6.   *SH*, p. 35. This sequence is nicely summarized by Peter Swales in "Freud, Breuer, and the Blessed Virgin."

gain clues about what sorts of questions to ask her during the evening self-hypnosis (and let us note here that, contrary to what Freud claimed and others have repeated,[7] hypnotic induction was never used during the actual "talking cure" itself). One after another, the symptoms disappeared, until the patient finally decided that her treatment would be completed on June 7, 1882, exactly one year after her confinement by Breuer. On that day, she reproduced a hallucination that she had experienced one night in July 1880 while caring for her father, and which had been at the root of her symptoms. Now, after carefully rearranging the room to match her father's, she relived the night when, literally paralyzed and struck mute by fright, she saw a black snake slithering toward him with the intention of

---

7. Thus, among other, similar versions: "Breuer arrived at a new method of treatment. He put her [Anna O.] into deep hypnosis and made her tell him each time what it was that was oppressing her mind" (S. Freud, *An Autobiographical Study* [1925], *SE* XX, p. 20). In reality, it was not Breuer but Freud himself who, bolstered by the hypnotic experiments of Charcot, Janet, and Delboeuf, first used direct hypnosis in order to recover and "talk away" traumatic memories. As for Bertha Pappenheim, she had no need of Breuer in order to get into a state of self-hypnosis, a fact made clear by this description of Breuer's "very simple" induction technique, "arrived at empirically": "The change-over from one state to another occurred *spontaneously* but could also be very easily brought about by any sense-impression which vividly recalled the previous year. One had only to hold up an orange before her eyes (oranges were what she had chiefly lived on during the first part of her illness) in order to carry her over from the year 1882 to the year 1881" (*SH*, pp. 36, 33; my emphasis). Freud's account tends to reinterpret Bertha Pappenheim's treatment in terms of the *medical* hypnosis of the 1890s, whereas the treatment actually belongs to a previous period in the history of hypnosis, when the *patient* directed the cure.

biting him: "In this way, [. . .] the whole illness was brought to a close. [. . .] [A]fter the reproduction [of the original scene] she was able to speak German. She was moreover free from the innumerable disturbances which she had previously exhibited. After this she left Vienna and travelled for a while; but it was a considerable time before she regained her mental balance entirely. Since then she has enjoyed complete health."[8]

---

8. *SH*, pp. 40–41.

CHAPTER THREE

Kreuzlingen

Everything—the whole enterprise of modern psycho-therapy—starts from this marvelous tale of Breuer's, almost too good to be true. And it isn't true. In the early 1970s, the historian Henri Ellenberger, curious about what eventually had become of Bertha Pappenheim, managed to determine that Breuer and the patient's family had placed her in the Bellevue Sanatorium at Kreuzlingen, Switzerland, where she was a patient from July 12, 1882— barely a month after the end of her treatment—until the following October 29. Her file contains a very interesting report from Breuer to the director, Robert Binswanger (father of Ludwig), as well as a second report, dated Octo-ber 1882, from the sanatorium's Dr. Laupus.[1] The report by Laupus wastes no words in establishing that Bertha Pappenheim has been suffering for six months from a

---

1. The two reports are reproduced in Part V of *JB*, pp. 276–292.

serious "trigeminal neuralgia," which itself has brought about the patient's addiction to the high doses of morphine that Breuer has been administering to dull her pain (Breuer was also giving her chloral to help her sleep).[2] This facial neuralgia, which Breuer mentions nowhere in the *Studies on Hysteria* (he likewise refrains from any mention of Bertha's embarrassing morphine addiction), appeared briefly in the spring of 1880[3] and played only "a quite subordinate role" in Bertha's illness until "the middle of March" 1882, when, quite possibly as a result of surgery performed in February on the patient's upper left jaw, the pain became "persistent and very excruciating."[4] The patient's pain has persisted throughout her stay at Kreuzlingen, Laupus notes, and all attempts to break her addiction to morphine have been utter failures, despite some apparent success at the very beginning of treatment. Dr. Laupus also reports that the patient has continued to exhibit "genuine signs of hysteria,"[5] moving from depressive states (during the day) to playful ones (in the evening) to "dramatic" enactments

---

2. *JB*, pp. 290–291.

3. Breuer's report, in *JB*, p. 278.

4. Letter from Bertha's mother to Robert Binswanger, dated August 27, 1882, and reproduced in *JB*, pp. 301–302. The role that this apparently bungled dental surgery played in Bertha's facial neuralgia has been pointed out by Fritz Schweighofer, who quite rightly deduces (as Breuer himself also seems to have done) that these pains were not hysterical in nature, even if Bertha did immediately integrate them into the panoply of her other symptoms (see Fritz Schweighofer, *Das Privattheater der Anna O. Ein Emanzipazionsdrama* [Munich-Basel: Ernst Reinhardt Verlag, 1987], pp. 75 sq., 107–108, 149); I thank Peter Swales for bringing this book to my attention.

5. *JB*, p. 291.

in her "private theater"[6] to intermittent loss of German (at night, as soon as her head hits the pillow).

Albrecht Hirschmüller, following up on Ellenberger's research, was able to dig up other documents from the Bellevue Sanatorium, among them a "report" written in English by Bertha Pappenheim herself, in which she complains of periods of "timemissing." There are also letters from Breuer to Robert Binswanger that show Breuer making preparations for his patient to go to Kreuzlingen. In one, dated November 4, 1881—immediately after the patient's return from the first sanatorium, at the point where the "talking cure," according to the *Studies*, had rendered her condition "bearable, both physically and mentally"[7]—Breuer writes that the attempt to acclimate Bertha to her family "will probably fail,"[8] and that it will be best to prepare for her immediate hospitalization. In another letter to Binswanger, from mid-June 1882 (only a few days after Bertha's allegedly definitive "cure"), Breuer states that Bertha is "very agitated," adding, "Today, the patient is suffering from slight hysterical insanity, confessing at the moment to all kinds of deceptions, genuine or not, occasionally still seeing bits of nonsense such as people spying on her, and the like, and exhibiting perfectly odd behavior on visits."[9] Other archival documents

6. *JB*, p. 292.
7. *SH*, p. 32.
8. *JB*, p. 292.
9. *JB*, pp. 294, 293. This letter, written between June 13 and June 16, 1882 (*JB*, p. 415, n. 240), followed an exchange of telegrams between Breuer and Binswanger on the subject of the "pressing decision" to hospitalize

unearthed by Hirschmüller demonstrate beyond a doubt that Bertha Pappenheim's symptoms, both somatic (neuralgia, morphine addiction) and functional, persisted well after her discharge from the sanatorium at Kreuzlingen. Indeed, between 1883 and 1887, Bertha made at least three prolonged visits to the same sanatorium in Inzensdorf where she had first been confined in 1881, and the doctors reached the same diagnosis every time: "hysteria."[10]

Breuer, who declined to resume treating Bertha Pappenheim after her stay at Kreuzlingen,[11] could not have had any illusions about the results of Anna O.'s "talking cure," especially since he had kept in touch with the Pappenheim family and enjoyed ample opportunity to inquire after his patient. We can easily understand, then, why he refrained for thirteen years from talking publicly about this "cure," and why he "at first [...] objected vehemently"[12] to the idea of doing so when Freud brought it up. If Freud was ultimately able to prevail, it was certainly less because of his powers of persuasion than because of the fact that Bertha Pappenheim, toward the end of the 1880s, had gradually recovered and, starting in the early 1890s, took up the literary and philanthropic activities that were to make her a pioneer of

---

Bertha, and so we see that Breuer did not long entertain his illusions (if indeed he had any) concerning the "cure" of June 7.

10. *JB*, p. 115.

11. See the letter dated October 7, 1882, from Bertha Pappenheim's mother to Robert Binswanger: "I should also have to accept a doctor in Vienna, since Dr. Breuer is unable to take over the treatment" (*JB*, p. 304).

12. *An Autobiographical Study, SE* XX, p. 21.

feminism and social work in Germany.[13] Obviously, without this unexpected recovery—which owed nothing whatsoever to the "talking cure"[14]—it would have been impossible to ring down the curtain on a happy ending for this case history (too many people in Vienna knew the true identity of Fräulein Anna O.).

As for Freud, he was completely aware of the whole situation. We know from Freud's unpublished letters to his fiancée, Martha Bernays (letters cited by Jones in his biography), that Breuer first spoke to Freud about Bertha Pappenheim on November 18, 1882, making no attempt to conceal the disastrous outcome of the treatment[15]; and on August 5, 1883, Freud wrote to Martha: "Bertha is once again in the sanatorium in Gross-Enzensdorf, I believe.[16] Breuer is constantly talking about her, says he wishes she were dead so that the poor woman could be free of her suffering. He says she will never be well again, that she is completely shattered."[17] Moreover, because Martha

---

13. As we know from a letter sent by Freud to Fliess and dated June 28, 1892, it was only on this date that Breuer finally made up his mind to collaborate with Freud on what would become the *Studies on Hysteria*.

14. I insist on this obvious point, which the defenders of psychoanalysis continue to erase systematically. Thus Peter Gay, in his hagiography of Freud, recalls Bertha Pappenheim's brilliant career and, unperturbed, goes on as follows: "These achievements testify to a substantial measure of recovery, but Breuer, in *Studies on Hysteria*, compressed with little warrant a difficult, often disruptive time of improvement into a complete cure" (Peter Gay, *Freud: A Life for Our Time* [New York and London: Norton, 1988], p. 66). Nicely put—but the fact that there was no improvement to "compress" has been neatly swept under the rug.

15. Jones, *The Life and Work of Sigmund Freud*, 1, p. 225.

16. Freud confuses this sanatorium with the one at Inzensdorf, and Jones reproduces the error in his biography (*ibid.*, p. 225).

17. This citation comes from John Forrester, who in turn cites an English

Bernays maintained quasi-familial ties with Bertha Pappenheim[18] and saw her regularly, Freud could not have avoided hearing about the evolution of Bertha's illness. Martha (by then Martha Freud), in two letters to her mother from January and May of 1887, writes that her friend continues to suffer from hallucinations in the evenings.[19] Not that any of this deterred Freud, later on, from pressing Breuer to publish Bertha's case history, and thus to provide an a posteriori validation of Freud's own cases; nor did he scruple to make false claims for Breuer's "method," as early as 1888, by comparing it favorably to the treatment of hysteria by suggestion: "It is even more effective if we adopt a method first practised by Josef Breuer in Vienna and lead the patient under hypnosis back to the psychical prehistory of the ailment and compel him to acknowledge the psychical occasion on which the disorder in question originated. This method of treatment is new [to riot in understatement, since at this point it has been used on precisely one patient],[20] but it produces successful cures [sic] which cannot otherwise be achieved."[21]

---

translation found in an unpublished manuscript written by Jeffrey Masson and deposited with the Sigmund Freud Copyrights at Wivenhoe (John Forrester, "The True Story of Anna O.," *Social Research*, 53, 2 [Summer 1986], p. 341).

18. Bertha Pappenheim's father was named legal guardian for Martha Bernays after her own father's death in 1880 (cf. Jensen, *Streifzüge durch das Leben von Anna O./Bertha Pappenheim*, p. 35; and Swales, "Freud, Breuer, and the Blessed Virgin").

19. Jones, *The Life and Work of Sigmund Freud*, 1, p. 225.

20. As far as we know, Freud's use of the cathartic method dates from 1889 (cf. Swales, "Freud, His Teacher, and the Birth of Psychoanalysis," p. 33).

21. "Hysteria" (1888), *SE* I, p. 56.

Obviously, after an advertising campaign like this one, there could be no question of pulling Anna O.'s case off the shelves, particularly since the timing of Bertha Pappenheim's treatment offered the not inconsiderable advantage of being able to claim victory in the race to beat Bourru and Burot, Delboeuf, and Janet to market (if not to the printer's). Freud, never ceasing to find fault with the cathartic method's disappointingly temporary results, nevertheless went on over the years proclaiming Anna O.'s "successful cure"[22] from the rooftops, describing it as a "great therapeutic success"[23]: "The patient had recovered and had remained well and, in fact, had become capable of doing serious work."[24]

Compare these effusions to the attitude, clearly less enthusiastic, of this success story's heroine. According to Dora Edinger, "Bertha Pappenheim never spoke about this period of her life and violently opposed any suggestion of psychoanalytic therapy for someone she was in charge of, to the surprise of her co-workers."[25] But her opposition was not the product of ignorance, for surely she had read the *Studies on Hysteria* and kept abreast of Freud's work.[26] It isn't hard to understand why Bertha

---

22. S. Freud, *Introductory Lectures on Psychoanalysis*, *SE* VI, p. 257.

23. S. Freud, "Two Encyclopedia Articles: (A) Psycho-analysis" (1923), *SE* VIII, p. 235.

24. *An Autobiographical Study*, *SE* XX, p. 20.

25. Dora Edinger, *Bertha Pappenheim, Freud's Anna O.* (Highland Park, Ill.: Congregation Solel, 1968), p. 15.

26. Statement by Dora Edinger, recorded by Lucy Freeman in her novelistic biography of Bertha Pappenheim, *The Story of Anna O.* (New York: Walker & Co., 1972), p. 203.

Pappenheim chose, in the face of all this, not to reveal the truth, and even to kick over the traces of her treatment with Breuer.[27] Now that she was a public figure with political battles on her hands, she must have been loath to supply her adversaries with the ammunition of her own florid hysteria and drug addiction. Which makes it all the easier to imagine the feelings that the erstwhile "Anna O." must have harbored toward the doctors who banked on her silence while they made their theoretical fortune: one word from her would have been enough to blow the whole fraud sky high.

---

27. Here again is Dora Edinger: "I think it is quite possible that she destroyed all documents referring to her early breakdown and requested her family in Vienna not to give out information after her death" (*Bertha Pappenheim, Freud's Anna O.*, p. 20).

CHAPTER FOUR

Constructions

The Pappenheim affair, carefully concealed from the public, seems nevertheless to have been an open secret among psychoanalytic insiders. As early as 1916, in his book *The History and Practice of Psychoanalysis*, Poul Bjerre noted almost in passing, "I can add that the patient was to undergo a severe crisis in addition to what was given out in the description of the case. Since then, however, she has lived, and still lives, in the best of health and in widespread activity."[1] And Carl Jung, in a private seminar of 1925, went even farther. Referring to confidential remarks made by Freud about the "untrustworthiness" of some of his early case histories, Jung stated: "Thus again, the famous first case that he [Freud] had with Breuer, which

---

1. I quote from the English translation of Bjerre's book (Boston: R. G. Badger, [1916] 1920), p. 86 (this passage is also mentioned by Peter Swales in "Freud, Breuer, and the Blessed Virgin").

has been so much spoken about as an example of a brilliant therapeutic success, was in reality nothing of the kind."[2] In fact, so little does the whole business appear to have been a secret within Freud's inner circle that Marie Bonaparte, upon returning from Vienna, where Freud had told her "the Breuer story," noted in her diary on December 16, 1927, *"The rest is well known*: Anna's relapse, her fantasy of pregnancy, Breuer's flight."[3]

It wasn't until 1953—some sixty years after Breuer's initial publication—that Ernest Jones, with the first volume of his biography of Freud, rattled the skeleton in the psychoanalytic closet. And, conveniently, this noise was drowned out by one that was even more sensational. According to Jones, Freud privately confided to him (as he had to Marie Bonaparte) that Breuer developed an intense countertransference to Bertha Pappenheim, which not only made his wife jealous but also, at the end of the treatment, resulted in an episode of pseudocyesis (hysterical childbirth), "the logical termination of a phantom pregnancy."[4] Breuer, the story goes, frightened at having the sexual nature of Bertha's illness so abruptly exposed, and hoping to calm her down, hypnotized her and then

2. Carl Gustav Jung, *Analytical Psychology: Notes of the Seminar Given in 1925*, ed. William McGuire (Princeton: Princeton University Press [Bollingen Series XLIX], 1989), p. 16.

3. My emphasis; archival document kindly provided by Elisabeth Roudinesco. For the circumstances surrounding the discovery of this document, see Appendix 1, as well as Elisabeth Roudinesco's *Présentation* in Henri F. Ellenberger, *Médecines de l'âme. Essai d'histoire de la folie et des guérisons psychiques* (Paris: Fayard, 1995), p. 15.

4. Jones, *The Life and Work of Sigmund Freud*, 1, p. 224.

fled in a "cold sweat."[5] He left Vienna the next day for a second honeymoon in Venice, where he played his part in producing his wife's actual pregnancy with their youngest daughter. And meanwhile poor Bertha, abandoned by her phantom lover, was forced to content herself with fulfilling her sterile fantasy of maternity by becoming the "'Mother' of an orphan institution."[6] The subtext of this tale is that Bertha Pappenheim's botched treatment was due to a serious underestimation of the role that sexuality played in her case, as well as to insufficient analysis of the transference and the countertransference. Breuer had failed, for want of courage and determination, where Freud doubtless would have triumphed. The failure belonged to Breuer, not to psychoanalysis. *Q.E.D.*

A lovely story, and one that has thoroughly made the rounds—but here again, careful research by Ellenberger, Hirschmüller, and Swales shows that this ingenious

---

5. *Ibid.*, 225. (How did Jones know about this interesting detail?)

6. *Ibid.*, p. 224. This explanation of what became of Bertha Pappenheim had already been put forward by Freud himself, if Peter Swales's notes on Marie Bonaparte's journal are to be believed (for the circumstances in which these notes were taken, see Appendix 1): "With glee, Freud told Marie Bonaparte what Anna O. was now doing—running a girls' home and campaigning against prostitution—all a preoccupation with sexuality!" (see p. 77). In his *Introductory Lectures on Psychoanalysis* Freud expressed this idea in somewhat more veiled terms: "Breuer's first hysterical patient was [. . .] fixated to the period when she was nursing her father in a serious illness. In spite of her recovery, in a certain respect she remained cut off from life; she remained healthy and efficient but avoided the normal course of a woman's life [and here, a footnote is added by James Strachey: "Anna O. was never married"]" (*Introductory Lectures on Psychoanalysis*, SE XVI, p. 274). If Freud discreetly wedged his foot in the door, countless psychoanalysts since then have

explanation of Bertha Pappenheim's failed treatment doesn't hold up. Mathilde Breuer probably *was* offended by the intense "rapport" that developed between her husband and his patient, but it simply isn't true that Breuer forsook Bertha for a hasty flight to Venice with his wife. Quite the opposite: Breuer arranged, very professionally, for his patient's transfer to Binswanger's sanatorium and then continued to work normally until he left to spend the summer with his family at Gmunden. Nor is the rest of the story true: Dora Breuer was born on March 11, 1882, three months before her alleged conception in Venice[7]; and Breuer's custom when a patient needed sedation was not to induce hypnosis but to administer injections of morphine or chloral.[8]

---

been kicking it wide open—Richard Karpe, for example, who uninhibitedly interprets Bertha Pappenheim's fight against prostitution as a sublimation of her aversion to Freud's sexual theories (Richard Karpe, "The Rescue Complex in Anna O.'s Final Identity," *Psychoanalytic Quarterly* 30 [1961], p. 23). It seems that the psychoanalysts, to judge from this brilliant interpretation, have never really forgiven Bertha Pappenheim for managing to recover without them.

7. Breuer's close relatives immediately pointed this error out to Jones, but apparently he saw no need to correct it in the second edition, despite his promise to do so. In this connection, see the letter from Hanna Breuer to Ernest Jones, dated April 24, 1954: "My sister-in-law Käthy Breuer in London told me in a recent letter that Ilse Hellman has been in touch with you about the error concerning Dora Breuer, and that you were quite willing to accept corrections before the imminent issue of a second edition of your book" (Centre Ellenberger, Paris; I thank Sonu Shamdasani for calling my attention to this very telling document, reproduced in its entirety in Appendix 2; the original has been deposited with the Jones Archives of the Institute of Psycho-Analysis, in London, where access to it is restricted).

8. For a good summary of all the contradictions in Jones's story, see *JB*, pp. 128–131.

As for the juiciest part of this story, the pseudocyesis, or hysterical childbirth, it is mentioned nowhere in Breuer's report to Binswanger, nor does it appear in Dr. Laupus's report or in letters sent to Binswanger by Bertha's mother and cousin; there is every reason to believe that it is sheer invention. Had the episode really taken place as Jones claims, Breuer's failure to mention this spectacular symptom to the colleague who was about to receive his patient would have been unthinkable. But here is what Breuer's report actually says: "The sexual element is *astonishingly underdeveloped*; I have never once found it represented even amongst her numerous hallucinations."[9] It is hard to see why Breuer, noted for his diagnostic skills, would have exposed himself to the indignity of having his medical opinion immediately contradicted by his patient's maternal-erotic delirium, and harder still to see why he would have taken such pains to assure Binswanger that Bertha was neither a liar

---

9. *JB*, p. 277 (my emphasis). In a preliminary report to Binswanger at the end of June 1882, Breuer presented his patient in the following way: "Fräulein Bertha Pappenheim, 23 years old, is convalescing from a very severe neurosis and psychosis of hysterical nature (*with no element of sexuality throughout the entire illness*)" (*JB*, p. 295; my emphasis). This asexuality, underlined by Breuer, conforms to what we know about what later became of Bertha Pappenheim, since she seems never to have had any love affairs. The only indication to the contrary is found in the acknowledgments that open Lucy Freeman's *The Story of Anna O*. Freeman relates in passing that her main informant, Dora Edinger, suggested that she refrain from using information provided by her "when a detail, *such as a reported romance in Bertha Pappenheim's early life*, could not be confirmed" (my emphasis). Freeman, reached by telephone (on December 12, 1994), verified that Dora Edinger did indeed make a vague remark along these lines but added that she immediately retracted it and did not allow Freeman to use this information in her book.

nor a malingerer:[10] in those days, he certainly would have aroused his colleague's suspicions of an affair between patient and doctor.[11] All the evidence indicates that the story peddled by Jones is a psychoanalytic myth based on rumor and professional gossip.

Who is the beneficiary of this myth? Because no one can still claim to be unaware that the official history of psychoanalysis is a vast anthology of tall tales, psychoanalysts customarily profess to be amused by Jones's "mistakes." But, here as elsewhere, Freud himself is to blame. There is no particular reason for believing that Jones unduly elaborated on the story Freud told him; after all, Freud was more than capable of embellishing the story himself. In fact, the pseudocyesis story has been handed down in a number of versions, which vary considerably according to when Freud told the story and to whom; taken together, they give the clear impression of being a spiteful piece of slander that was built up over a period of several years.

The version that most closely approximates the "classic" story told to Jones is found in a letter from Freud to Stefan Zweig dated June 2, 1932, which deserves to be quoted at some length: "What really happened with Breuer's patient I was able to guess (*erraten*) later on, long after the break in our relations, when I suddenly remem-

---

10. "Her present contention that her entire illness is an invention is quite definitely false, even if individual elements are not genuine" (*JB*, p. 295; translation modified).

11. Hirschmüller notes that in 1888, in similar circumstances, Breuer had duly informed Binswanger of the amorous feelings that a patient had toward him (*JB*, p. 140). Why, then, would Breuer have behaved any differently in the case of Bertha Pappenheim?

bered something Breuer had once told me in another context before we had begun to collaborate and which he never repeated. On the evening of the day when all her symptoms had been disposed of, he was summoned to the patient again, found her confused and writhing in abdominal cramps. Asked what was wrong with her, she replied: 'Now Dr. B.'s child is coming!'[12] At this moment he held in his hand the key that would have opened the 'doors to the Mothers,' but he let it drop. With all his intellectual gifts there was nothing Faustian in his nature. Seized by conventional horror he took flight and abandoned the patient to a colleague. For months afterwards she struggled to regain her health in a sanatorium. I was so convinced of this reconstruction (*Rekonstruktion*) of mine that I published it somewhere. Breuer's youngest daughter (born shortly after the above-mentioned treatment, not without signifi-

---

12. In a laudable effort to exonerate Freud, Lisa Appignanesi and John Forrester offer the hypothesis that the "Dr. B." mentioned in the letter to Stefan Zweig was not Breuer but his friend Dr. Breslauer, director of the Inzensdorf sanatorium: "We should always bear in mind that there were other doctors whose name began with B. whose baby it might have been, in particular Dr. Breslauer at the Inzensdorf Sanatorium, who treated Bertha over the next four years" (*Freud's Women*, pp. 488–489). But Appignanesi and Forrester are out of luck, since this hypothesis is tenable only for the published English translation of the letter to Stefan Zweig, where the phrase "Dr. B." is indeed distinguished from "Breuer," which, being spelled out, would seem to indicate that two different people are involved. In the original German version, however, there can be no doubt that we are dealing with Breuer, whose name Freud repeatedly abbreviates as "Br.," as he also does in the incriminating passage: "Jetzt kommt das Kind, das ich von Dr. Br. habe" (Stefan Zweig, *Briefwechsel mit Hermann Bahr, Sigmund Freud, Rainer Maria Rilke und Arthur Schnitzler,* herausgegeben von Jeffrey B. Berlin, Hans-Ulrich Lindken und Donald A. Prater [Frankfurt am Main: S. Fischer Verlag, 1987], p. 200).

cance for the deeper connections!) read my account and asked her father about it (shortly before his death). He confirmed my version, and she informed me about it later."[13]

In her diary, Marie Bonaparte mentions a story more or less identical to this one (we'll leave aside, for the moment, one crucial difference):

> The 16th of December [1927], in Vienna, Freud told me the Breuer story. [...] The rest is well known: Anna's relapse, her fantasy of pregnancy, Breuer's flight.
>
> Breuer's daughter questioned her father. He confessed everything that Freud had written in the *Selbstdarstellung*.
>
> Br[euer] a[n] Freud: Was haben Sie mir ja angestellt! [Breuer to Freud: "What have *you* got me into!"][14]

---

13. Ernst L. Freud, ed. *Letters of Sigmund Freud, 1873–1939* (New York: Basic Books, 1960), p. 266. Stefan Zweig, who gives the official version of the Anna O. episode in his book *Mental Healers* (New York: Viking, 1932, pp. 285–286), was related to the wife of Wilhelm Pappenheim, Bertha's brother (see Edinger, *Bertha Pappenheim*, p. 13, n. 1). Perhaps Freud, by telling Zweig the "unofficial" version of the story, was hoping to prevent the consequences of any possible leaks of information within the family.

14. Elisabeth Roudinesco, private archives; reproduced in Appendix 1, pp. 78–79. Compare this passage with the notes made from memory by Peter Swales after skimming through what seems to be a summary of the diary that Marie Bonaparte sent to Ernest Jones in June 1954: "After Freud had in 1914 [Swales's interpolation: *On the History of the Psycho-Analytic Movement*] published a more suggestive account of what really happened, Breuer's daughter asked her father about it; and one day Breuer came to see Freud, saying, 'What have you done to me!'" (see Appendix 1, p. 79). To my knowledge, Marie Bonaparte's diary is the only place where this visit and Breuer's outrage are mentioned. If the episode is anything other than Freud's invention, it seems to me that it must have taken place after the publication of *On the History of the Psycho-Analytic Movement*, where Freud first mentions the sexual component of Anna O.'s treatment, rather than after the appearance of the *Selbstdarstellung* (*An Autobiographical Study*), in February 1925, when Breuer, then eighty-three years old, was soon to die (June 20, 1925).

But attempts to locate the pseudocyesis story have turned up no trace of it in any of Freud's published works, so it is hard to see how Breuer could have confirmed a "reconstruction" of which he had no knowledge. As Hirschmüller notes,[15] Breuer's confirmation (if in fact there was one) could only have had to do with certain allegations made by Freud about Breuer's refusal to continue their collaboration. Indeed, from 1914 on, Freud had been attributing the break between them to Breuer's resistance to sexuality, insinuating on the basis of "indications," "interpretations," and "reconstructions"[16] that Breuer, at the end of Bertha Pappenheim's treatment, realized the sexual nature of "the very intense suggestive *rapport* with [his] patient"[17] but chose to "retire in dismay" rather than face this "love transference."[18] It is quite possible, of course, that Breuer did partially confirm this version of the story when questioned by his daughter. In fact, he seems never to have made any secret of the emotional complications in which Bertha Pappenheim's

---

15. *JB*, pp. 127 and 377, n. 299a (Hirschmüller refers here to Gerhard Fichtner, *"Freuds Briefe als historische Quelle,"* lecture delivered to the Second Conference of the Association Internationale d'Histoire de Psychanalyse, Vienna, July 21–23, 1988).

16. *On the History of the Psycho-Analytic Movement* (1914), *SE* XIV, pp. 11–12: "[. . .] this opposition between our views [. . .] had deeper causes, but [. . .] it was only later that I learnt from many clear indications how to interpret it"; "Breuer never said this to me in so many words, but he told me enough at different times to justify this reconstruction of what happened." See also *An Autobiographical Study*, *SE* XX, p. 26: "[. . .] I came to interpret the case correctly and to reconstruct, from some remarks which he had made, the conclusion of his treatment of it."

17. *On the History of the Psycho-Analytic Movement*, *SE* XIV, p. 12.

18. *An Autobiographical Study*, *SE* XX, p. 26.

treatment entangled him, even going so far as to describe it as a virtual "ordeal": "I swore at the time that I would *never* put myself through such an ordeal [*Ordal*] again."[19] But nothing in this statement justifies our leaping to the conclusion that Breuer admitted fleeing in terror from the uncontrollable eruption of a massive erotic transference. There is ample evidence that Breuer was perfectly capable of spotting the sexual element of his patients' hysteria,[20] and we have no reason not to trust him when he stresses Bertha Pappenheim's asexuality, "astonishing" in his eyes: "The case of Anna O., which was the germ-cell of the whole of psycho-analysis, proves that a fairly severe case of hysteria can develop, flourish, and be resolved without having a sexual basis."[21] It is easy to understand Freud's desire to turn these rather embarrassing statements by his former collaborator into signs of "resistance" and "repression." Nevertheless, Freud's rewriting of Anna O.'s story rests on sheer psychoanalytic *interpretation* (not to mention gossip),[22] and it can in no way stand as a

---

19. Letter from Breuer to Auguste Forel, dated November 21, 1907, cited in Paul F. Cranefield, "Josef Breuer's Evaluation of His Contribution to Psycho-Analysis," *International Journal of Psychoanalysis* 39 (1958), 5, p. 319.

20. See p. 27, note 11. Hirschmüller points out that Breuer shared the old medical prejudices about the relationship between sexuality and hysteria (*JB*, p. 108). Freud himself, in *On the History of the Psycho-Analytic Movement*, describes how Breuer told him about the link between hysteria and "*secrets d'alcôve*" (bedroom secrets). Compare also what Breuer wrote in the theoretical portion of the *Studies on Hysteria*: "I do not think I am exaggerating when I assert that *the great majority of severe neuroses in women have their origin in the marriage bed*" (*SE* II, p. 246; Breuer's emphasis).

21. Letter to Forel dated November 21, 1907, cited in Cranefield, "Josef Breuer's Evaluation," p. 320.

22. Here is yet another wild interpretation, contained in a letter from

factual account, no matter what Freud wanted his disciples and confidants to believe.

But Freud's disciples and confidants weren't universally taken in anyway. James Strachey, for example, to whom Jones sent a draft of his chapter on Breuer and Freud, seems to have had grave doubts about Freud's version of the story, as shown by this comment addressed to Jones on October 24, 1951: "Breuer's adventure. Freud told me the same story with a good deal of dramatic business. I remember very well his saying: 'So he took up his hat and rushed from the house.'—But I've always been in some doubt of whether this was a story that Breuer told Freud or whether it was what he inferred—a 'construction,' in fact." Jones made his unruffled reply three days later: "Freud gave me two versions of the Breuer story. The theatrical one about his grabbing his hat, and then the true one that Breuer hypnotized Anna and calmed her before leaving. I have left out the hat; 'rushed from the house' seems to me legitimate, since it conveys the spirit of the situation."[23] (The crimes committed in the name of spirit!)

In his biography of Freud, Jones claims that the story of the hysterical childbirth is corroborated by an unpublished letter from Freud (made available to him by his daughter, Anna) to Martha Bernays, dated October 31,

---

Freud to Jung, dated November 21, 1909: "*Chimney sweeping* [Bertha Pappenheim's synonymous expression for the "talking cure"] is an action symbolic of coitus, something Breuer certainly never dreamed of" (William McGuire, *The Freud/Jung Letters* [Princeton: Bollingen Series XCIV/Princeton University Press, 1974], p. 267).

23. Jones Archives, Institute of Psycho-Analysis, London.

1883: "Confirmation of this account may be found in a contemporary letter Freud wrote to Martha which contains substantially the same story."[24] Well, not quite—and Jones knew it. In fact, thanks to Peter Swales and John Forrester, who both managed independently to get hold of this letter,[25] we can now reconstitute the first version of the rumor that Freud started. Here is what he wrote to his fiancée: "It will surely interest you to know that your friend Bertha P. is doing well in the Enzensdorfer[26] institution, is getting rid of her pains and her morphine-poisoning, and is rapidly gaining weight. This I know from a colleague Sekundarius [Assistant], who is known there and who sometimes drives out there to

---

24. Jones, *The Life and Work of Sigmund Freud*, 1, p. 225.
25. Janet Malcolm tells how Peter Swales tricked Anna Freud into giving him access to a copy of the letter (*In the Freud Archives* [London: Jonathan Cape, 1984], pp. 131–132). As for John Forrester, he became aware of the correspondence between Freud and his fiancée at the Sigmund Freud Copyrights (Wivenhoe) when he consulted the manuscript of an appendix that Jeffrey Masson had been planning to add to his edition of the Freud-Fliess letters. In his manuscript, Masson quoted some unpublished letters from Freud to Breuer and to his fiancée, letters to which he enjoyed unlimited access while he still belonged to the Freudian inner circle. The absence of that appendix from Masson's edition of the Freud-Fliess correspondence is unexplained, but I see no reason to conclude that the owners of the letter from Freud to his fiancée simply "forgot" about it, as Forrester hastens to suggest in a footnote: "It is a mystery why this letter was not published in the original edition of Freud's correspondence, since it is of great historical and personal interest; the hypothesis of a general cover-up of the Freudian skeletons will not explain its omission, since all the important elements had been at least alluded to in Jones' account of his biography of Freud" (Forrester, "The True Story of Anna O.," p. 331). I confess that I am helpless to understand what evidence compels Forrester to make this assertion.
26. Inzensdorf (see p. 20, note 16).

substitute for Dr. Breslauer. He is very taken with the girl, with her piquant looks in spite of grey hair, her wit and her intelligence. I believe that, were it not that, as a psychiatrist, he knows so acutely what a cross [to bear] is the disposition to severe hysterical illnesses, he would have fallen in love with her. But discretion *all around*, Marty. Also in respect of what I tell you now. Breuer too has a very high opinion of her and has given up her care because his happy marriage threatened to come unstuck on account of it. The poor wife could not bear it that he devoted himself so exclusively to a woman, about whom he obviously spoke with much interest, and was certainly jealous of nothing else but the engrossment of her husband by a stranger. Not in the ugly, tormenting way, but in the quietly resigned manner. She fell ill, lost her spirits, until it dawned on him and he learned the reason for it, which of course was a command for him to withdraw completely from his activity as physician of B.P. Can you be silent, Marty? It is nothing dishonorable, but rather something very intimate and that one keeps to oneself and one's beloved. I know it of course from him personally; he seemed to hint that something about his staying away is circulating. I could not tell him what. You, my darling, will also not ask for it."[27]

---

27. Since I was unable to gain access to the German original, I quote Peter Swales's English translation of this letter (in "Freud, Breuer, and the Blessed Virgin"), which seems to me more reliable than Jeffrey Masson's translation as cited in John Forrester's article (besides, Masson does not cite the passage in its entirety). I thank Peter Swales for letting me use this letter, from which I draw the same conclusions that he drew.

The next exchange between Sigmund and Martha also deserves to be quoted, since it throws an interesting light on the subtext of this correspondence. On November 2, 1883, Martha responded to her fiancé's letter: "It has often been on the tip of my tongue to ask you why Breuer gave up Bertha. I could well imagine that those somewhat removed from it were wrong to say that he had withdrawn because he was unable to do anything for her. It is curious that no man other than her physician of the moment ever got close to poor Bertha, that is, when she was healthy she already [had the power] to turn the head of the most sensible of men—what a misfortune for the girl. You will laugh at me, dearest, I so vividly put myself in the place of the silent Frau Mathilde that I could scarcely sleep last night." Freud gave this response on November 4: "My beloved little angel, you were right to expect that I would laugh at you. I do so with great gusto. Are you really so vain as to believe that people are going to contest your right to your lover or later to your husband? Oh no, he remains entirely yours, and your only comfort will have to be that he himself would not wish it any other way. To suffer Frau Mathilde's fate, one has to be the wife of a Breuer, isn't that so?"[28]

What can we conclude from this correspondence, kept so long from the public eye? One thing seems clear: Breuer, like many other doctors in similar circumstances,

---

28. Since these two letters are not reproduced in Peter Swales's paper, I cite Jeffrey Masson's translation, which appears in Forrester, "The True Story of Anna O.," pp. 331–333.

got his wings singed in this contact with a florid hysteric. Fritz Schweighofer calculates that, over the period of a year and a half, Breuer spent more than a thousand hours in Bertha's company.[29] In the first half of the nineteenth century, the era of magnetic cures, a therapeutic marathon like this one wasn't unusual, though we can imagine how, late in the century, it might have alarmed Breuer's wife and provoked some juicy rumors among his colleagues. But is that any reason to swallow these rumors and imagine, as Mathilde Breuer and Martha Bernays did, a love affair, even a Platonic one, between Josef and Bertha? Since Freud's time, we have grown so used to interpreting any therapeutic relationship, especially hypnotic rapport, in terms of "transference *love*" that the idea seems self-evident to us (even critical minds like Swales and Schweighofer subscribe to it). But what, after all, makes us so sure? Who, besides Freud and the psychoanalysts, says that hypnosis and the doctor-patient relationship are all about sex and libido? The fact is, the "paradigmatic" case of Bertha Pappenheim and Josef Breuer, so frequently cited in support of this theory, gives us nothing but vague rumors, which even Freud at the time judged too improper to bring up with his friend. But Freud later used the very same rumors to shore up his own interpretation of the whole episode, and he's lucky Breuer didn't sue him for defamation of character. A good lawyer, in two minutes flat, would have ripped Freud's malicious "reconstructions" to shreds.

---

29. Schweighofer, *Das Privattheater der Anna O.*, p. 78.

When did Freud begin to spread the pseudocyesis tale? We really don't know, but it seems to have started off as a piece of psychoanalytic gossip for internal consumption only and, as such, removed from any need for verification, and subject to all sorts of modifications and additions. Thus Jones, in his biography of Freud, tells how Breuer, "some ten years" after the end of Bertha Pappenheim's treatment, called Freud in on a case of hysteria. Before the two of them went in to see the patient, according to Jones, Breuer "described her symptoms, whereupon Freud pointed out that they were typical products of a phantasy of pregnancy. The recurrence of the old situation was too much for Breuer. Without saying a word he took up his hat and stick and hurriedly left the house."[30] Jones cites this anecdote, supplied by Freud, as additional confirmation of the pseudocyesis story, but we might do well to wonder whether this anecdote actually gave rise to that story in the first place. Let's play Freud's game for a moment and, reconstruction for reconstruction, imagine the following sequence:

1. "Some ten years" (or, more likely, thirteen to fourteen years) after the end of Bertha's treatment, Breuer finds himself beginning to be seriously irritated by Freud's mania for interpreting absolutely everything in sexual terms, and perhaps some gesture of his betrays his irritation.

---

30. Jones, *The Life and Work of Sigmund Freud*, 1, p. 226 (where we find the reappearance of the hat that Jones discreetly omitted from his version of the pseudocyesis episode: nature abhors a vacuum).

2. Freud, stung, hastens to read Breuer's gesture of irritation as resistance to his interpretation (as indeed Freud is beginning to do more and more when others disagree with him).

3. Freud makes the connection between Breuer's "resistance" and what he knows about the termination of Bertha's treatment, and on this basis he brilliantly deduces the scene of hysterical childbirth.

Unlikely? Far-fetched? Maybe—but no more improbable than Freud's own "reconstruction," based as it is on mere presumption. Originally, it may have been just one more analytic *Konstruktion* of the kind he engaged in every day with his patients. But did he begin, like a mythomaniac, to fall for his own story? To Jung, whose account is far too often overlooked, Freud was soon confiding that he himself had witnessed Bertha's transferential delirium: "Freud told me that he was called in to see the woman the same night that Breuer had seen her for the last time, and that she was in a bad hysterical attack, due to the breaking off of the transference."[31] We know this isn't true, of course, since the documents cited by Jones establish that

---

31. Jung, *Analytical Psychology*, p. 16. This seminar of Jung's, given in 1925, had been privately published and circulated within the Jungian milieu. Jones, while he was working on his biography of Freud, took care to avoid getting in touch with Jung (and earned Jung's reproach) but may have heard about this seminar from a follower of Jung's with whom he was in contact, the psychiatrist Eddie Bennet (information kindly provided by Sonu Shamdasani).

only in November 1882 did Freud first hear Breuer talk about Bertha Pappenheim's treatment.[32]

It gets better. In 1985, in the *New York Times*, the journalist Daniel Goleman reported on remarks made by Frank Hartman, a psychoanalyst who claimed to have access to Marie Bonaparte's unpublished (and closely guarded) journal. Goleman, paraphrasing Dr. Hartman, wrote: "Freud told the Princess that one of the reasons Josef Breuer, his first collaborator, stopped treating his famous patient Anna O. was that Breuer had become so infatuated with his patient that his wife, out of jealousy, attempted suicide—a fact never before brought to light."[33] Given Dr. Hartman's failure to produce any documents, however, his account could not be verified until Elisabeth Roudinesco, on the basis of information provided by Peter Swales and myself, finally tracked the relevant passage down in Marie Bonaparte's journal: "The 16th of December [1927], in Vienna, Freud told me the Breuer story. His wife tried to kill herself toward the end of Anna/Bertha's treatment. The rest is well known."[34]

Did Jones have access to this latest fish story of Freud's? According to Daniel Goleman, Hartman claims

---

32. See also Freud's letter of July 8, 1915, to James J. Putnam: "I was never Breuer's assistant, never saw his famous first case, and only learned of it years later from Breuer's report" (Ernst L. Freud, ed., *Letters of Sigmund Freud* [New York: Basic Books, 1960], p. 309). To complicate matters even more, this last claim contradicts Freud's letters to Martha, cited by Jones.

33. In Daniel Goleman, "Freud's Mind: New Details Revealed in Documents," *New York Times*, November 12, 1985, p. C5.

34. See Appendix 1.

that Marie Bonaparte did make her journal available to Jones,[35] and this statement is confirmed by her letter to Jones dated June 18, 1954, where she announces that she is sending him a selection of passages from her diary to help him with his biography of Freud.[36] This important document is now gone from the Institute of Psycho-Analysis in London, but we can reasonably suppose that the Princess did include the passage on Mathilde Breuer's suicide attempt, a sensational scoop by comparison with the version of the story that Jones had published in the first edition of the biography, the year before. In the later editions, however, Jones scrupulously avoids any mention of this rumor propagated by Freud—a rumor formally refuted, as Jones could not have failed to notice, by Freud's letter to Martha of October 31, 1883. Thus the published version of the pseudocyesis story, outlandish as it is, is also a piously censored version of an even wilder, crazier story.

Were there other versions as well? One thing is certain: Freud, interpreting the "Pappenheim affair" according to his own immediate needs, finally lost sight of the facts. But who even cares, in the unreal, derealized universe of psychoanalysis, where interpretation passes for reality and fiction is taken for truth?[37] There is no Freudian

---

35. Goleman, "Freud's Mind," p. C5 .
36. Jones Archives, Institute of Psycho-Analysis, London (see Appendix 1).
37. A good example of this is the recent "revision" of the Anna O. case that Moustapha Safouan offers in response to Ellenberger's article. Not content simply to retell the mythical version of the pseudocyesis story challenged by Ellenberger, Safouan shores up his own Lacanian interpretation of the case with an episode that Lucy Freeman clearly

historiography, only mythography. The pseudocyesis, constructed of clues, rumors, and lies, was not a fantasy of Bertha Pappenheim's. It was Freud's fantasy, a pseudomemory meant to explain away, after the fact, the abysmal failure of the original "talking cure."

---

invented for her novelistic account of Bertha Pappenheim's life. Safouan writes: "When [Anna O.'s] health once again improved, thanks again to the healing power of Eros, Breuer, apparently making a paternal gesture, hoped to make her happy by inviting her on an automobile ride to the Prater one sunny day in May [...]. He asked his second child, Bertha, then six years old, to go along. To these two Berthas was added Breuer's mother, also named Bertha. Breuer's desire could not have been more clearly revealed: If the one you love is named Bertha, what can you ask her for, if not another Bertha?" (Moustapha Safouan, *"L'Histoire d'Anna O.: Une révision,"* in *Le Transfert et le désir de l'analyste* [Paris: Le Seuil, 1988], pp. 19–20). Here, Safouan no doubt means to illustrate the well-known Lacanian maxim that "truth has a structure of fiction."

CHAPTER FIVE

The 1882 Report

As Henri Ellenberger notes concisely, "The famed prototype of a cathartic cure was neither a cure nor a catharsis."[1] It can be objected that this early setback doesn't necessarily invalidate the curative powers of narration and memory, first observed in Bertha Pappenheim's treatment. After all, the "talking cure" definitely did produce some sort of outcome, if a temporary one. The psychoanalyst Moustapha Safouan, after citing Ellenberger's statement in his "revision" of the case of Anna O., goes on to say, "Undeniably, though, Bertha Pappenheim's condition did improve at a certain point in her treatment."[2] Or, to put it another way, didn't Bertha Pappenheim do better whenever she could talk about the origin of her symptoms?

---

1. Ellenberger, "The Story of Anna O.," p. 279.
2. Safouan, *Le Transfert et le désir de l'analyste*, p. 11.

Yes—and no. When we examine the case history published in 1895, or especially the initial report of 1882, we see that the theme of memory emerged only gradually over the course of treatment. For the first four months, Bertha Pappenheim gained relief by telling fairy tales of her own invention. Over the next two months, the same effect was obtained through her recounting—or, more precisely, acting out ("tragedizing")[3]—morbid hallucinations. Only after August 1881was the "talking cure" directed toward her recounting the memories that supposedly were at the root of her symptoms.[4] Therefore, we have no grounds for assuming that the temporary remission of Bertha Pappenheim's symptoms owed more to her remembering their origin than to her telling fairy tales or even, as Lacan would have it, to her "verbalizing" her hallucinations instead of acting them out, since each of these procedures finally had the same effect. Peter Swales puts it very well: "the cathartic treatment, involving a detailed biographical accounting for the symptoms, exerted an essentially *placebo* or *suggestive* effect."[5]

Remembering and narration, obviously, were only two elements among others involved in what amounted to a negotiation of symptoms between Breuer and his patient: "You give me this, and I'll give you a symptom." Thus Breuer, in the sanatorium at Inzensdorf, literally had to beg Bertha and recite a ritual phrase in English ("And

---

3. *Tragieren*: Breuer uses this verb in the published case history (see p. 13, note 4), as well as in his original report (*JB*, pp. 285 and 414, n. 215).

4. Cf. *JB*, p. 288.

5. Swales, "Freud, Breuer, and the Blessed Virgin."

there was a boy") before she would agree to begin telling her purgative stories. She also insisted on feeling Breuer's hands, to make sure it was really he.[6] As Henri Ellenberger has aptly pointed out, the treatment of Bertha Pappenheim bears an unmistakable resemblance to courses of magnetic treatment from the late eighteenth and early nineteenth centuries, whereby patients prescribed for themselves the therapeutic procedures that would heal them and accurately predicted the moment of their own healing.[7] What real difference is there between the extravagant demands of a Bertha Pappenheim and those of a Joly, the patient whose cataleptic attacks could be made to stop only when his doctor, the Marquis de Puységur, followed the patient's orders and burst into song, accompanying himself on the harp?[8] And what about the demands of Fredericke Hauffe, the famous "Seeress of Prevorst," who had Justinus Kerner cure her by building a "nerve tuner" (*Nervenstimmer*)? Or those of Estelle, Despine's little paralytic, who would not walk unless her doctor-magnetist applied gold to her body?[9] It is impossible to escape the feeling that Anna O.'s stories and "reminiscences" also participated in this type of therapeutic bargaining, and

6. *JB*, p. 287.
7. Henri F. Ellenberger, *The Discovery of the Unconscious: The History and Evolution of Dynamic Psychiatry* (New York: Basic Books, 1970), p. 484; "The Story of Anna O.," p. 279.
8. Armand Marie-Jacques de Chastenet, Marquis de Puységur, *Mémoire pour servir à l'histoire et à l'établissement du magnétisme animal* (Toulouse: Privat, 1986; reprint of the 1786 edition), p. 133.
9. On the magnetic treatment of Fredericke Hauffe and Estelle L'Hardy, see Ellenberger, *The Discovery of the Unconscious*, pp. 79–81, 129–131.

that her treatment would have been just as effective no matter what procedure had been used.

Breuer, in fact, in his original report of 1882, has nothing at all to say about "memories" or "reminiscences" (by contrast with what he would have to say in 1895); he speaks only about "*caprices*" (in French) and "fantasies." What is even more striking is that these two terms make their appearance just at that point in the report where Breuer mentions the episode in which Bertha's hydrophobia was cured, an episode described in the *Studies* as the true beginning of the "talking cure," centered as it was on memories of *actual* traumatic events. In the 1882 report, however, this episode is immediately preceded by what Breuer, in a charming phrase, calls Bertha's "stocking *caprice*": "When she was awoken and put to bed in the evening, the patient could not bear her stockings being removed; only on awakening at 2 or 3 o'clock would she occasionally do this, complaining at the same time of the impropriety of allowing her to sleep with her stockings on. One evening she told me a true story of long ago, how at night time she would creep in to eavesdrop on her father (at that time, night nurses could no longer put up with her), how she slept in her stockings for this reason, then on one occasion she was caught by her brother, and so on. As soon as she had finished she began to cry out softly, demanding why she was in bed with her stockings on. Then she took them off, and that was the last we saw of the stocking caprice."[10]

---

10. *JB*, p. 288

Is it any wonder that Breuer, in the *Studies on Hysteria*, chose to pass over this first miraculous "healing" in silence and substitute the story about the governess's horrid little dog? Nor could Bertha's nocturnal discovery by her brother easily be made to pass for the kind of "psychic trauma" that Freud and Breuer had in mind in 1895. Not only that, the stocking symptom and its disappearance had an aspect of *literal* "capriciousness" that was altogether too obvious for Breuer even to think about parlaying this comical episode into the inaugural event of the cathartic cure.

In reality, the 1882 report shows clearly that Breuer was still quite far from theorizing about the Pappenheim case in terms of psychic trauma or memories dissociated from consciousness. Here, for instance, is what Breuer says about the "talking cure": "It was clear from this work as a whole that each product of her abnormal activity, whether it was *a spontaneous product of her phantasy* or derived from the diseased part of her psyche, acted as a psychic stimulus, and continued to act until it was narrated, but with this it completely lost its potency."[11] And elsewhere, on the subject of a "whim" of Bertha's, which consisted of her asking for bread and then refusing to eat it, he writes: "This was a purely psychic inhibition proceeding from one of her phantasies, and when she *narrated the phantasy* the inhibition was discarded."[12]

But, better yet, here is what Breuer has to say, at the

---

11. *Ibid.*, p. 288 (my emphasis).
12. *Ibid.*, p. 289 (my emphasis).

end of the report, about the fourth period of Bertha Pappenheim's illness, when she supposedly was reliving events from the corresponding days of the previous year: "At the end of December, at the time of the Jewish Christmas, she was particularly disturbed; [she] recounted nothing new in the evenings [. . .], but only the *phantasy stories* which she had told day by day during the 1880 festival, when dominated by extreme anxiety. Considerable relief at the end of this series."[13] Nowhere in his report does Breuer mention any actual events of the year before, nor does he mention the diary kept by Bertha's mother, which allegedly confirmed the astounding accuracy of Bertha's "reminiscences." The closest Breuer comes is in a passage of the short preliminary report that he sent to Robert Binswanger at the end of June 1882, where he writes elliptically: "During the past six months, her actions were influenced day by day by the events of the same day in the previous year. With the help of a vivid sense impression connected with the former (last year's) events she was able invariably to project herself completely into the situation of the previous year, even to the extent of having hallucinations"[14] (Breuer is probably alluding here to his practice of showing Bertha an orange in order to transport her back to the year before). But Breuer's final report leaves no doubt about the imaginary nature of these "events": what Bertha had been reproducing with such stunning accuracy was not the *events* of

---

13. *Ibid.*, pp. 289–290 (my emphasis).
14. *Ibid.*, p. 295.

the preceding year but rather the *stories she told Breuer* during her trancelike states. In other words, Bertha, by entering a self-induced hypnotic state, was able to reproduce the self-hypnosis and reveries of the corresponding day of the preceding year (perhaps with the help of some private diary kept day to day?). Bertha Pappenheim's famous "memory" was actually the memory of previous hypnotic states (an "alternating memory," to use Pierre Janet's term).[15]

Clearly, then, the theme of pathogenic memory was introduced into the Bertha Pappenheim case only later on, to make it fit the theory of traumatic hysteria put forward by Charcot and the Salpêtrière school, a theory that Breuer and Freud had adopted in the meantime. Freud, in the context of his squabble with Janet over who came first, was often to claim that Breuer had made his discovery "in 1881, independently of any outside influence"[16]— that is, before Charcot's investigations into traumatic hysteria and the continuation of those investigations by Janet in *L'automatisme psychologique* (1889). But this statement

---

15. Pierre Janet, *L'automatisme psychologique. Essai de psychologie expérimentale sur les formes inférieures de l'activité humaine* [Psychological Automatism] (Paris: Société Pierre Janet/CNRS, 1989; reprint of the 1889 edition), pp. 88 ff.

16. "A Short Account of Psycho-Analysis" (1923), *SE* XIX, p. 193. In the article "Psycho-Analysis (Freudian School)" (1926), which appeared in English in the *Encyclopaedia Britannica*, Freud likewise writes, "This was at a date before the investigations of Charcot and Pierre Janet into the origin of hysterical symptoms, and Breuer's discovery was thus entirely uninfluenced by them" (*SE* XX, p. 262). See also the 17th *Introductory Lecture on Psychoanalysis*, where Freud, after conceding that Janet did publish earlier than Breuer, slips in this low blow: "America is not named after Columbus" (*SE* XVI, p. 257).

is demonstrably false, at least if we consider the actual theoretical content of the "discovery," since no trace of the theory of the "mechanism of hysteria," as proposed by Breuer and Freud in the "Preliminary Communication" of 1893, can be found in the report of 1882.[17] In fact, no theory can be found there at all: Breuer speaks rather vaguely about the elimination of "psychic excitation" due to "fantasies," and that's all. At any rate, there is no mention of "psychic trauma," "dissociation of consciousness," or "reminiscence."[18]

The claim that it was Breuer who discovered the role of psychic trauma in hysterical neuroses is actually a total (and self-serving) anachronism on Freud's part, for the theory set out in the *Studies on Hysteria* comes straight from Charcot, as well as from other French works in this area. Breuer could not have known about these works at the time, for the simple reason that they were published only after the treatment of Bertha Pappenheim. Where,

---

17. In *An Autobiographical Study*, Freud relates that Breuer finally agreed to publish the "Preliminary Communication" because "in the meantime, Janet's works had anticipated some of his results, such as the tracing back of hysterical symptoms to events in the patient's life, and their removal by means of hypnotic reproduction *in statu nascendi*" (*SE* XX, p. 21).

18. Freud knew exactly what he was doing, since he more than likely had access to Breuer's report, which Robert Binswanger had returned to Breuer after making a copy for his own archives. Poul Bjerre, who must have obtained his information from Freud himself, writes: "For private reasons Breuer, however, did not go any further in his following out of the beginning he had made. He even let his notes lie untouched upon his desk. And they would probably still be lying there, if he had not come into a dispute about the thing with his younger colleague Freud" (*The History and Practice of Psychoanalysis*, p. 86).

then, does the idea of "psychic trauma" come from? It comes from the notion of shock, in the most literal sense of the term. The history of trauma as a concept begins with the spectacular train wrecks of the second half of the nineteenth century, with all the commotion they caused (in this connection, Wolfgang Schivelbusch speaks of a "European railroad trauma").[19] Some of the victims suffered concussions, developed different kinds of paralysis, or became aphasic or amnesiac.[20] Others, with no apparent physical injuries, developed analagous symptoms, often after a fairly long incubation period, and when these victims sued the railroads' insurance companies, physicians were brought in to offer expert testimony on this strange (and somewhat suspect) phenomenon.

Only at the beginning of the 1880s was a psychopathological explanation beginning to be proposed for the "nervous shock" caused by these Industrial Age accidents

---

19. On the history of the concept of traumatic neurosis, see Wolfgang Schivelbusch, *The Railroad Journey: Trains and Travel in the 19th Century* (New York: Urizen Books, 1979), p. 127 (my thanks to Hal Foster, who brought this book to my attention). See also Esther Fisher-Homberger, *Die Traumatische Neurose. Vom somatischen zum sozialen Leiden* (Vienna: Hans Huber Verlag, 1975); Mark S. Micale, "Charcot and *Les Névroses traumatiques*: Historical and Scientific Reflections," *Revue Neurologique* 150 (1994), 8–9, pp. 498–505.

20. It is still in this sense of concussion that Freud uses the word "trauma" in his article "Amnesia," which appeared in 1893–94 in *Diagnostisches Lexikon für präktische Ärtzte*, edited by Anton Bum and Moritz Schirner: "There have certainly been cases recorded in which the patient, after a trauma (*Trauma*) of the skull with brain damage, became amnesiac for a longer period of his past life" (article rediscovered and presented by Oswald Ulrick Kästle in *Psyche* 41 [1987], 6, p. 520; translation by Richard Skues, whom I thank for bringing this text to my notice).

(until then, the talk had been of microscopic injury to the spinal cord—"railway spine"—resulting from the intensity of the mechanical blow). The first mention of the idea that symptoms observed after an accident might be due to psychological shock or trauma, itself caused by fear, appears in Herbert Page's *Injuries of the Spine and Spinal Cord Without Apparent Mechanical Lesions and Nervous Shock, in Their Surgical and Medico-Legal Aspects* (1883), and this is the idea that Charcot began to develop at the Salpêtrière, starting in 1885. Demonstrating that hypnotic suggestion could artificially bring about different types of hysterical paralysis that were completely analogous to the types resulting from accidents, Charcot made the striking inference that posttraumatic cases of paralysis were due to an "autosuggestion" implanted in the psyche during the quasi-hypnotic state created by fear and psychic shock: "because of the annihilation of the *ego* produced by hypnotism in the one case, and, as one may suppose, by the nervous shock in the other, that idea [the "autosuggestion," or *idée fixe*] once installed in the brain takes sole possession and acquires sufficient domination to realise itself objectively in the form of paralysis."[21] Clearly, it was only a short step from here to the thought that hysterical states in general were caused by emotional shocks, memories of which remained as *idées fixes* in a hypnoid "unconscious" or "subconscious,"

---

21. Jean-Martin Charcot, *Clinical Lectures on Diseases of the Nervous System*, vol. III, (London: The New Sydenham Society, 1889), p. 305.

and that such memories could be acted on by way of hypnosis. That step was quickly taken by Janet, Binet, Bourru and Burot, Delboeuf . . . and Freud,[22] who during his stay in Paris, between 1885 and 1886, had attended Charcot's demonstrations of posttraumatic hysterical disorders. The complete psychologization of "nervous shock" had begun, and with it the ever more exhaustive hunt for unconscious traumatic memories.

It seems that Freud, for his part, made the connection very early between these French investigations and the Pappenheim case. In the 1888 article "Hysteria," as we have seen, he was already citing the "method initially used by Josef Breuer," and he added: "It is the method most appropriate to hysteria, because it precisely imitates the mechanism of the origin and the passing of these hysterical disorders. For many hysterical symptoms, which have resisted every treatment, vanish spontaneously under the influence of a sufficient psychical motive (for instance, a paralysis of the right hand will vanish if in a dispute the patient feels an impulse to box

---

22. Janet, *L'Automatisme psychologique*, 1889; Alfred Binet, *Les Altérations de la personnalité* (Paris: Alcan, 1892); Henri Bourru and Prosper Burot, *Variations de la personnalité* (Paris: Baillière, 1888); Joseph Delboeuf, *Le Magnétisme Animal: A propos d'une visite à l'Ecole de Nancy* (Paris: Alcan, 1889). For the likely influence of Bourru and Burot on Freud, see Léon Chertok, "A propos de la découverte de la méthode cathartique," *Bulletin de psychologie*, 5 November 1960, pp. 33–37; Léon Chertok and Raymond de Saussure, *Naissance du psychanalyste* (Paris: Payot, 1973), pp. 155–56 and 222. For Delboeuf's and Janet's influence, see Malcolm Macmillan, "Delboeuf and Janet as Influences in Freud's Treatment of Emmy von N.," *Journal of the History of the Behavioral Sciences* 15 (1970), pp. 299–309.

his opponent's ear) or under the influence of some moral excitement or of a fright."[23] It is easy to see here how Freud literally projected onto Breuer's case his brand-new knowledge from the Salpêtrière, making Bertha Pappenheim's treatment the prototype of the experimental treatment that he would conduct the following year on Anna von Lieben (Cäcilie M.) and Fanny Moser (Emmy von N.).

The problem, however, was that this prototype, which his patients immediately and obligingly confirmed,[24] simply never existed except in Freud's own mind (and, later, in the mind of Breuer, who seems to have been persuaded by Freud to adopt, retrospectively, Freud's own rereading of the case). It was not just that Bertha Pappenheim had not been cured of her symptoms at the end of the treatment; Breuer himself, at the time, was nowhere near conceptualizing the stories that his patients told him in terms of "traumatic memories." Only in 1895, when the Pappenheim case had to be made to fit in with other cases presented in the *Studies*, did Breuer systematically convert his patient's "fantasies" into "reminiscences" of traumatic and shocking events. The case of Anna O., far from being the empirical origin of Freud's and Breuer's new theory of hysteria, came to illustrate it after the fact, through a self-serving revisionism that was anything but innocent. What a fine example of

---

23. "Hysteria," *SE* I, p. 56.
24. It is impossible not to be impressed by the regular avalanche of "traumas" put forward by Fanny Moser and Anna von Lieben from the middle of 1889 on.

Nachträglichkeit (Freud's "aftermath-effect"): modern psychotherapy, with its emphasis on the curative powers of narration and memory, has as its founding narrative the biased rewriting of an older narrative, one that tells only made-up stories. And what should we find but a false memory right at the heart of the modern myth of remembering.

CHAPTER SIX

Carl Hansen

An objection can be raised: these stories, imaginary or not, were still narratives, and Bertha Pappenheim's "talking cure" did develop, after all, in the direction of narrated memories. Where did this increasing emphasis on remembering come from? If Charcot's trauma theory was not yet available to Breuer, doesn't that prove that the "talking cure" really was spontaneous and genuine?

This objection is a solid one, and it finds support in Breuer's own statements. In a letter to Forel dated November 21, 1907, Breuer writes: "The case which I described in the *Studies* as No. 1, Anna O., passed through my hands, and my merit lay essentially in my having recognized what an important case chance had brought me for investigation, in my having persevered in observing it attentively and accurately, and my not having allowed any preconceived opinions to interfere with the simple observation of the important data."[1] Breuer's modesty, false or not, shouldn't deceive us. Even if he still had no knowledge of Charcot's work on traumatic hysteria, he certainly had his own theoretical assumptions, and there is every reason to believe that these, especially his belief in hypnotic hypermnesia, are what gradually directed Bertha Pappenheim's treatment toward the excavation of "memories."

Contrary to what is usually assumed, when Breuer met Bertha Pappenheim he was not exactly uninformed about hypnosis, as Hirschmüller has established: not only did Breuer, a physiologist, have an interest in animal hypnosis (in 1897, he was still talking about "hypnoid states" in pigeons), he was also aware of the hypnotic treatments for hysteria that were being carried out in Vienna by his colleague and friend Moriz Benedikt.[2] Yet Breuer, like others, as the historian Uffe Hansen has shown more recently, would have maintained only a marginal interest in hypnosis had it not been for the decisive impetus lent to the study of hypnotic phenomena by the demonstrations of the Danish stage hypnotist Carl Hansen.[3] Surely it was no coincidence that Bertha Pappenheim's illness and/or treatment should have begun at the end of 1880. Indeed, Hansen

---

1. In Cranefield, "Josef Breuer's Evaluation of His Contribution to Psycho-Analysis," p. 319.

2. *JB*, pp. 93–95 and 364–365, n. 48.

3. On Carl Hansen and his role in the treatment of Bertha Pappenheim, see Uffe Hansen's excellent book, *Hypnotisøren Carl Hansen og Sigmund Freud* (Copenhagen: Akademisk Forlag, 1991), on which I have drawn freely in the writing of this chapter. See also the section titled "The Hansen

gave performances at Vienna's Ringtheater in January and February of that year, after his triumphant tour of Germany had attracted the interest of such prominent scientists as Fechner, Zöllner, Preyer, Wundt, Möbius, and Heidenhain. Hansen's demonstrations of catalepsy, muscle spasms, negative hallucinations, and posthypnotic amnesia created a stir that quickly developed into an outright scandal.

As Fritz Schweighofer tells the story, early in 1880 Vienna was gripped for several months by a "veritable attack of mesmero-hypnotic fever."[4] People flocked to the Ringtheater; whole salons were succumbing to

---

Phase" in Alan Gauld's *A History of Hypnotism* (Cambridge: Cambridge University Press, 1992), pp. 302 ff.; and Edward Shorter, *From Paralysis to Fatigue: A History of Psychosomatic Illness in the Modern Era* (New York: The Free Press, 1992), pp. 150–154.

4. Schweighofer, *Das Privattheater der Anna O.*, p. 95. As we know, Freud later declared that he had become convinced of the reality of hypnotic phenomena during one of Hansen's performances (*An Autobiographical Study, SE* XX, p. 16). Nevertheless, in a letter to his friend Eduard Silberstein, dated February 3, 1880, he writes (in English): "I have made up my mind to stay at home and work to let Mr. Hansen puzzle our dear fourteen friends, as he can. I am almost sure the interruption of evening might put me out and destroy my artificial systematic structure of study. Let my Mr. Hansen come when I am rather more independent and give him my best love. Hope you will keep your mind sceptical and remember 'wonderful' is an exclamation of ignorance and not the acknowledgement of a miracle" (Walter Boehlich, ed., *The Letters of Sigmund Freud to Eduard Silberstein, 1871–1881* [Cambridge: The Belknap Press of Harvard University Press, 1990], p. 177). Hansen's performance of February 3 (attended by Archduke Albrecht) ended in a huge uproar when one of the human guinea pigs brought up from the audience claimed to have faked being hypnotized. Did Freud decide at some point in the following two weeks to go and judge for himself, in spite of his upcoming exams? Or is this story from *An Autobiographical Study* just one more example of Freud's bragging, meant to establish his place among the pioneers of hypnotic phenomena?

hypnosis, and children were hypnotizing one another in the schoolyards. In the local papers, people unburdened themselves of opinions on charlatanism and fakery, and Hansen struck back by filing suit (unsuccessfully) against one of his accusers. Other citizens—like Moriz Benedikt, following the example of Heidenhain, who had given a lecture on the topic[5]—attempted to put together a "physiological" explanation for the miracles wrought by Hansen. The philosopher Franz Brentano, shaken in his conviction that there could be no such thing as unconscious psychic phenomena, made a special trip to Breslau on February 8 to see Heidenhain and be reassured by the noted physiologist himself. There was also some anxiety about the risks to Hansen's audiences, particularly in connection with the dangers posed by a stunt known as "the human plank," in which Hansen would balance a cataleptic person over the backs of two chairs and then climb on top of his human guinea pig. The police, after consulting the Viennese Medical Faculty, finally put a stop to Hansen's performances on February 18.

Even if Bertha Pappenheim never attended any of Hansen's performances in person, it would have been all

---

5. Rudolf Heidenhain, *Der Sogenannte thierische Magnetismus. Physiologische Beobachtungen* (Leipzig: 1880). This volume reproduces a lecture that Heidenhain delivered in Breslau on January 19, 1880 (scarcely two weeks after his first encounter with Hansen and hypnotic phenomena), which was published three weeks later in the *Wiener medezinische Blätter*, nos. 7–9, 12–26 February 1880—that is, in the midst of all the controversy surrounding Hansen. For more on Heidenhain, see Roger Smith, *Inhibition, History and Meaning in the Sciences of Mind and Brain* (London: Free Association Books, 1992), pp. 125–129; Marcel Gauchet, *L'Inconscient cérébral* (Paris: Gallimard, 1992), pp. 116–117.

but impossible for her not to have heard about them, if not in the newspapers then by word of mouth. And that goes double for Breuer, who was a personal friend of both Benedikt and Brentano, and who certainly wouldn't have missed an opportunity to bring himself up-to-date on the physiological interpretation of hypnosis that his eminent colleague Heidenhain had proposed. It's no great surprise, then, as Uffe Hansen points out, if at the end of 1880 Bertha Pappenheim was developing symptoms that, feature for feature (intractable contractures, localized anesthesia, posthypnotic amnesia, positive and negative hallucinations, visual disturbances, aphasia,[6] and so on), resembled those produced during Hansen's staged demonstrations. These striking "symptoms," which were to make a partial reappearance in the Salpêtrière hysterics, could all be found in the bag of tricks elaborated by stage hypnotists and other "electro-biologists" in England, where Hansen had been staying from 1870 to 1875.[7]

---

6. Following up on his investigations into the phenomena to which Hansen had introduced him, in the *Breslauer ärtzliche Zeitschrift* of February 28, 1880, Heidenhain published an article, *"Halbseitiger Hypnotismus. Hypnotische Aphasie* [Hypnotic Aphasia]. *Farbendblindheit und Mangel des Temperatursinnes bei Hypnotischen"* (my emphasis). Bertha Pappenheim's language problems began with an episode of aphasia.

7. It may have been through Hansen that this Anglo-Saxon hypnotic tradition entered France, where Hansen was staying in 1875 and had contact with the Salpêtrière, according to an interview he gave in 1889 to *Tidsskrift for Magnetisme* (cited by Uffe Hansen, *Hypnotisøren Carl Hansen*, p. 70). We cannot help noting, along with Uffe Hansen, that 1875 was also the year when the physiologist Richet, then an intern at the Salpêtrière, published his article *"Du somnambulisme provoqué,"* which was to inspire Charcot's interest in hypnotic phenomena.

As for the other phenomena displayed by Bertha Pappenheim (dual personality, her "speaking in tongues," her selective rapport with Breuer, the "talking cure," hypnotic hypermnesia), they all belonged to the array of magnetic treatments current in the Germany of the early nineteenth century. Countless somnambulists, from the depths of their magnetic "second lives," had already been prophesying, speaking in tongues, and reliving the past for the benefit of the magnetists with whom they were in magnetic rapport.[8] The similarity between Bertha Pappenheim's treatment and the older magnetic cures has often been noted,[9] even if no one has been able to come up with a satisfactory answer to why this tradition should have resurfaced in the middle of positivist Vienna, within a medical community where the very existence of "animal magnetism" was already long forgotten. But Carl Hansen's stay in Vienna appears to be that answer. Indeed, Uffe Hansen has managed to

---

8. Onno van der Hart and his collaborators have turned up two examples of magnetic treatment in Holland (one conducted in 1813, the other between 1850 and 1851), which, like Bertha Pappenheim's treatment, were based on the remembering or reliving of past traumatic events (Vijselaar and van der Hart, "The First Report of Hypnotic Treatment of Traumatic Grief," art. cited; Onno van der Hart and Kees van der Velden, "The Hypnotherapy of Dr. Andries Hoek: Uncovering Therapy Before Janet, Breuer and Freud," *American Journal of Clinical Hypnosis* 29, 4 (April 1987). Likewise, in E.T.A. Hoffmann's *The Magnetizer*, Theobald heals his beloved Augusta by getting her to relive, under the influence of magnetism, a significant experience from their childhood.

9. Among various candidates for the role of Bertha Pappenheim's model, we have the "Seeress of Prevorst" and Clemens Brentano's Catherine Emmerich (Ellenberger), Father Blumhardt's Gottliebin Dittus (Hirschmüller), the stigmatic Louise Lateau (Swales), and Despine's little Estelle (Schweighofer).

establish that Carl Hansen—from a theoretical perspective, by way of Brandis[10]—was a direct heir of the German magnetic tradition, and that he had an exchange on this subject with Benedikt, one of the few Vienna physicians who stayed in touch with that tradition.[11] Obviously, it doesn't take much for the thought to arise that Benedikt, in the context of the commotion stirred up by Hansen, might have talked about all of this with his friend Breuer, and that Breuer in turn unwittingly allowed it to affect the course of Bertha Pappenheim's treatment. What seems particularly likely is that the increasing emphasis on the past over the course of the treatment corresponded to Breuer's interest in hypnotic hypermnesia, a topic on which Benedikt had presented a

---

10. J. D. Brandis, *Über psychische Heilmittel und Magnetismus* (Copenhagen: 1818).

11. Benedikt mentions that he read Ennemoser in his youth, as well as Reichenbach's "*Odisch-magnetische Briefe*"; cf. Moriz Benedikt, *Hypnotismus und Suggestion* (Leipzig–Vienna: Breitenstein, 1894), p. 17. These older works may have been what prompted Benedikt, in the mid-1860s, to begin using hypnosis (or "catalepsization," as he preferred to call it) in the treatment of hysteria (Benedikt, among others, attempted to cure the future psychoanalyst Rudolph von Urbantschitsch's mother of sleepwalking). As Ellenberger points out (*The Discovery of the Unconscious*, pp. 46, 301, 486, 523, 536, 764), Benedikt stressed the role of the "pathogenic secret" (often, he said, of a sexual nature) in the genesis and treatment of hysterical disorders. Breuer and Freud, in their "Preliminary Communication" of 1893, wrote, without further elaboration, "We have found the nearest approach to what we have to say on the hysterical and therapeutic sides of the question in some remarks, published from time to time, by Benedikt" (*SH*, p. 8). And in his "Theoretical," included in *Studies on Hysteria*, Breuer refers elliptically to "some interesting communications" of Benedikt's that appear in *Hypnotismus und Suggestion* (*SH*, p. 210); in one such "interesting communication," Benedikt says he cured an adolescent girl's hysterical symptoms by getting her to talk about having being raped at the age of seven.

lecture ("Catalepsy and Mesmerism") to the Viennese Society of Physicians on March 3, 1880.[12]

Hypermnesia is one of the oldest stars in the magnetic tradition's firmament. Throughout the nineteenth century, magnetists were reporting their patients' amazing feats of memory (as American hypnotherapists do today). Some patients could recite whole passages from books. Others spoke languages forgotten since childhood, vividly recalling past events and even past lives. Still others remembered (as Bertha Pappenheim also did) everything that had taken place during previous somnambulistic states, events of which they retained no memory in their normal waking state. (This last phenomenon, which quickly came to be known as "double consciousness," was certainly at the root of these various myths: the belief in somnambulistic *hyper*mnesia is only the mirror image of the belief in postsomnambulistic *a*mnesia, which itself was already a time-honored feature of demonic possession.[13]) Benedikt, in his lecture, never

---

12. Moriz Benedikt, "*Über Katalepsie und Mesmerismus*," originally published in the *Wiener medizinische Blätter*, 1880, 10, pp. 250–252 (text cited and commented on by Uffe Hansen, *Hypnotisøren Carl Hansen*, pp. 123–126; Appendix 3 of the present volume contains an English translation of Benedikt's text). In *Hypnotismus und Suggestion* (pp. 28–40), this lecture is reproduced in its entirety (but, it appears, with some noteworthy revisions) under the title *"Der psychologische Werth der Katalepsierung."*

13. As early as the late 1880s, Bernheim and Moll were pointing out that the posthypnotic amnesia reported by hypnotic subjects was itself "a result of hypnotic training" (Albert Moll, *Hypnotism* [1889]; English translation [New York: Charles Scribner's Sons, 1894], p. 139) and could be easily removed by countersuggestions. Thus there is nothing really extraordinary about the fact that hypnotized subjects were capable of remembering their previous hypnotic states, since they probably had

denied the existence of hypnotic hypermnesia. He simply gave it a resolutely physiological explanation (as others, such as Carpenter and Braid, had done before him), without invoking the "clairvoyance" so dear to the magnetists of old.

As Heidenhain had already done, Benedikt compared "animal magnetism" to an "artificial catalepsy," noting that "cataleptic persons are capable of reproducing to perfection long series of acoustic impressions in a foreign language, received in a quite passive fashion years before,"[14] and he explained this fact by the brain's capacity to retain virtually anything: "*The human brain is a phonograph*"; "*[t]he human brain is a photographic plate.*"[15] Thus the vaunted "clairvoyance" of magnetized subjects, far from being the manifestation of some supranormal capacity, would appear to rest on a natural hypermnesia, a mechanism normally inhibited by the brain's superior functions. Therefore, Benedikt claimed, the miraculous self-diagnoses of somnambulists are in fact *memories* of diagnoses observed unconsciously in the past, and somnambulists' astonishing linguistic feats are based on *memories* of foreign languages heard in childhood. In the same vein, Benedikt's 1894 book relates his encounter with

---

never forgotten them in the first place. For a good update on the myths surrounding these topics, see the articles collected by Helen Petinati in *Hypnosis and Memory* (New York: The Guilford Press, 1988). For a history of the medical-legal debates on this question, see Jean-Roch Laurence and Campbell Perry, *Hypnosis, Will and Memory* (New York: The Guilford Press, 1988).

14. Benedikt, *"Katalepsie und Mesmerismus,"* p. 250.
15. Benedikt, *Hypnotismus und Suggestion*, p. 82 (Benedikt's emphasis).

Carl Hansen during the hypnotist's stay in Vienna. Benedikt asked Hansen whether he had ever witnessed magnetized subjects who spoke or sang in languages that they didn't know in the waking state. Indeed Hansen had, and he proceeded to tell Benedikt about hypnotizing a British officer in Africa one day, who suddenly began to sing in a strange language that no one present knew: "Then I said to Hansen that it was Welsh and, surprised, he told me that this is exactly what it had turned out to be. I tapped Hansen on the shoulder and said, 'See my visionary gift? I can even see what happened in Africa years ago!'"[16]

It is easy to understand how this positivist explanation of hypnotic phenomena might have seemed so seductive and interesting to a physiologist like Breuer, who had already conducted experiments in animal hypnosis. Benedikt's materialistic, secular explanation, like the one that Heidenhain was proposing in Germany, essentially lent a new respectability to the rather disreputable "animal magnetism" of the poets and charlatans. In particular, Benedikt's use of the notion of hypermnesia cleared the way for an apparently objective approach to hypnotic phenomena by dispelling the aura of fraud and fakery that had kept physicians from taking these phenomena seriously: "Doubtless the imagination and the will can call forth cataleptic states; still, it makes no sense

---

16. "Das Auftachen von Hansen," in *Hypnotismus und Suggestion*, pp. 26–27. (Jones recounts the same episode, with all the embellishments we have come to expect, in *The Life and Work of Sigmund Freud*, 1, pp. 251–252.)

to suppose that a serving girl who wants to simulate catalepsy can recite long Bible passages in their original language, copy foreign writing with exactitude and speed, [. . .] solely as a result of her willed simulation."[17] Nevertheless, this translation of "clairvoyant" phenomena into the language of unconscious memory did nothing to challenge the idea of hypermnesia itself. Benedikt, purportedly offering a positivist explanation for the marvels claimed by the magnetists, actually gave them his scientific blessing. From that point on, the whole paraphernalia of "clairvoyance" could be recycled under the label "hypermnesia."

Bertha Pappenheim got the point, it seems. Who can really believe that her "gift of tongues," developed over the course of her treatment, made its appearance through the agency of the Holy Ghost (or, what am-

---

17. Benedikt, *"Katalepsie und Mesmerismus,"* p. 251. Benedikt is referring here to a story (or myth) that authors of the period often cited in illustrating the possibility of unconscious psychic phenomena. Maudsley, who attributes the story to Coleridge (whereas Benedikt attributes it to Forbes Winslow; cf. *Hypnotismus und Suggestion*, pp. 31–31), reconstructs it as follows: "There are other stories on record, like that of the servant girl which Coleridge quotes who, in the ravings of fever, repeated long passages in the Hebrew language, which she did not understand, and could not repeat when well, but which, when living with a clergyman, she had heard him read aloud" (Henry Maudsley, *The Physiology and Pathology of the Mind* [New York: D. Appleton and Co., 1867], p. 15). The story is also related by Albert Moll in *Hypnotism*, p. 126. And Brentano, writing in 1874, twice quotes Maudsley's passage in refuting the notion that Coleridge's story proves the "existence of unconscious ideas" (Franz Brentano, *Psychology from an Empirical Standpoint* [New York: Humanities Press, 1973], pp. 59, 112; Brentano's work is cited by Peter Swales in "Freud, His Teacher, and the Birth of Psychoanalysis," p. 39). Thus Benedikt's example is far from neutral; it refers to a debate already under way, about the existence of a psychic unconscious.

ounts to the same thing, a "demonic" unconscious)?[18] The phenomenon is so similar to examples of hypermnesia given in Benedikt's lecture that suspicion points to Breuer's contamination of the treatment. If Bertha Pappenheim was able to produce "with an extraordinary fluency, [...] an admirable extempore English translation" of the French and Italian books she was reading, or if "she used Roman printed letters, copying the alphabet from her edition of Shakespeare,"[19] these feats were probably more the effect of Breuer's theoretical expectations than of Bertha's "excellent memory"[20] or linguistic gifts (which Breuer greatly exaggerated anyway, to judge from the number of Germanisms that pepper the "report" she wrote in English at Kreuzlingen). The same goes for Bertha's self-prescribed treatment, a typical feature of magnetic "clairvoyance" that Benedikt had also discussed in his lecture, once again attributing this feature to "photographic" memories of previous medical attention.

As for the stress laid on remembering, an emphasis that increased as the treatment progressed, the odds are that it

---

18. Like amnesia and anesthesia, "speaking in tongues" had long been considered an objective criterion for demonic possession. A clear connection exists between nineteenth-century somnambulists and "dual personalities," on the one hand, and their "possessed" counterparts of earlier times, on the other. (One of the very first cases of "dual personality," studied by Eberhardt Gmelin in 1789, concerned alternation between a German personality and a French one.)

19. *SH*, p. 26.

20. See the 1882 report: "Considerable intelligence; *excellent memory*, remarkably shrewd powers of reasoning and clear-sighted intuition" (*JB*, p. 277; my emphasis).

was a direct result of Breuer's interest in hypermnesia. And, indeed, it is difficult to see how Breuer could have resisted the temptation of putting Benedikt's hypotheses to the test with the "spontaneous" somnambulist Bertha Pappenheim by asking her about her past from time to time. Even if Breuer, when he eventually wrote his report, decided to treat his patient's memories as imaginary (before he changed his mind yet again, under Freud's influence), he still probably began by interpreting Bertha's pronouncements as actual "photographic" reproductions, in Benedikt's sense. The grotesque (if not downright silly) age regression claimed by Bertha Pappenheim during the fourth phase of her treatment corresponds too closely to Benedikt's theory of "clairvoyance" not to arouse the suspicion of a hoax, or at least a folie à deux, between doctor and patient. What the fascinated Breuer was observing was ultimately nothing but the reflection of his own hypotheses: a photographic plate.

CHAPTER SEVEN

Retrospective Hallucination

Having come this far, I have to face one last (and predictable) objection: How could Bertha Pappenheim's symptoms have been brought about by Breuer's suggestions alone, since she was already ill before he was called in? To put it another way, did Breuer infuse the Pappenheim case with Benedikt's hazy theories, or did I?

At first glance, this objection looks unanswerable. In reality, though, it rests on an illusion created by the chronological mode of exposition that Breuer uses in the *Studies*. Indeed, he begins by referring to what he calls the "incubation period" of Bertha Pappenheim's illness, a period toward the end of which he was called in to treat her lingering cough. If Breuer is to be believed, it was during this incubation period that Bertha Pappenheim began to develop various symptoms under the impact of certain traumatic events, such as her hallucination of the black snake. And here we should pay attention to the term *incubation,* which is no accidental product of Breuer's pen: Charcot, in his lectures, had already stated that in cases of posttraumatic hysteria, symptoms often appear after a variable "incubation" period in which the memory of the initial trauma is subject to "unconscious elaboration."[1] This theory, which was to form the starting point for Freud's later speculations on the "aftermath-effect" (*Nachträglichkeit*), and which we are seeing again today in formulations about Post-Traumatic Stress Disorder (PTSD) and Multiple Personality Disorder (MPD), amounts to the assertion that hysteria has a kind of secret life. (This theory would have proved quite expedient whenever an explanation was needed for why an injured worker, or a soldier wounded in the war of 1870, had taken months, years, even a decade or longer to develop symptoms of hysteria.)

Breuer went quite a bit farther than Charcot, however: in the case of Bertha Pappenheim, not only the ideas associated with the trauma but also the *symptoms themselves* supposedly carried on this subterranean existence. A close reading of her 1895 case history reveals, surprisingly, that *no one close to Bertha Pappenheim noticed any of the symptoms from the so-called incubation period.* But, if we can believe the "reminiscences" that Breuer obtained during

---

1. See, for instance, Appendix I to his *Clinical Lectures on Diseases of the Nervous System,* vol. III, p. 387: "It is worthy of remark that in the case of Le Log—, as in others of the same kind, the paralysis was not produced at the very moment of the accident, but it was only after an interval of several days, after a sort of incubation stage of unconscious mental elaboration." Freud and Breuer both refer repeatedly to Charcot on this point; cf. *SH,* pp. 134, 213, 220, and elsewhere.

the fourth phase of the illness, Bertha's symptoms at this time—deafness, episodes of fainting, trancelike states ("*absences*"), nausea, muscular and glottal spasms, visual disturbances—were not symptoms that would have been easy to hide. More than once, it seems, Bertha had even lost the ability to speak: "She lost the power of speech (a) as a result of fear, after her first hallucination at night, (b) after having suppressed a remark another time (by active inhibition), (c) after having been unjustly blamed for something and (d) on every analogous occasion (when she felt mortified)."[2] And yet at no time throughout this period did anyone around Bertha Pappenheim notice anything at all: "No one, perhaps not even the patient herself, knew what was happening inside her [*in ihr*]."[3] (Perhaps it wasn't Bertha herself but those in her inner circle who were suffering from negative hallucinations.)

Breuer's 1895 account of the case discreetly glosses over this surprising blindness, suggesting only that his patient's numerous symptoms during her illness's incubation period were something that "happen[ed] inside her." But he was much more forthcoming in his 1882 report: "I

---

2. *SH*, p. 40; and, more generally, pp. 36–40. The context makes it clear that all these symptoms supposedly belonged to the "incubation period," for Breuer says that they were recapitulated "in reverse order, starting before the time when the patient became bed-ridden" (p. 35). And likewise: "Since this laborious analysis of her symptoms dealt with the summer months of 1880, which was the preparatory period of her illness, I obtained complete insight into the *incubation and pathogenesis* of this case of hysteria" (p. 38; Strachey's translation omits Breuer's emphasis).

3. *Ibid.*, p. 23 (translation slightly modified).

recount the matter *as I learned it from her*; it can be verified only by comparison with details from other known dates, since there is general agreement. This part of her illness is altogether hidden from those around her. Even she herself, I believe, knows in detail only of such things *as I have told her according to her report under hypnosis, which we deal with later*."[4] Now it all makes sense: if Bertha's impressive symptoms went unnoticed within her circle, it was because they simply never revealed themselves—not "inside her," and not outside her, either. The so-called incubation period was a pure reconstruction of Breuer's, from stories that the patient told later on. And because these stories were obtained under hypnosis—that is, in a state known to increase suggestibility and imaginative activity, and this a good year after the treatment had begun—there can be no more room for doubt about the highly suspect nature of the "memories" cited by Breuer. All the evidence indicates that the "incubation period," far from preceding the treatment, was the product of progressive hypnotic coaching, and of what Bernheim would call a decade later a "retrospective hallucination" (the ancestor of the more recent "False Memory Syndrome"): "I have called *retrospective hallucinations*" Bernheim wrote, "memory-images that are created all of a piece in the mind of a subject, and that correspond to no reality. [. . .] I have shown that it is possible to make certain very suggestible subjects believe that they have witnessed a particular event or been actors or spectators in a particular situation; and the memory-

---

4. *JB*, p. 278 (my emphasis).

scene suggested to them, whether they are awake or asleep, arises in their minds as if it had actually taken place."[5] It's a good bet that Bertha Pappenheim's famous "traumatic" snake hallucination, which for Breuer marked the onset of her illness, was actually a "retrospective hallucination" of this kind.

And so it is unwise to ask Bertha Pappenheim's preexisting symptoms to scrub Breuer's treatment clean of any suspicion that it might have been based on hypnotic suggestion. The fact is, until Breuer diagnosed his patient as having a "hysterical" cough, she had not shown any hysterical symptoms at all. As soon as we've been cured of the retrospective hallucination induced by Breuer's story, we can't help seeing that he was brought in simply to treat a lingering cough—and nothing else. Here, moreover, is how Breuer himself presents the whole affair in his report of 1882: "I first visited the patient at the end of November on account of her cough. It was a clear case of tussis hysterica; *however*, I classified the patient immediately as mentally ill on account of her strange behavior."[6] Note the strangeness of this "however." It seems at first to contradict Breuer's reasoning—Why would Bertha Pappenheim be mentally ill *in spite of* being hysterical?—but makes perfect sense in the context of

---

5. Hippolyte Bernheim, *Hypnotisme, suggestion, psychothérapie. Etudes nouvelles* (Paris: Doin, 1891), p. 124. On the question of the "falsifications of memory" (*Erinnerungs-fälschungen*) or "paramnesias" suggested by way of hypnosis, see also Auguste Forel, *Hypnotism or Suggestion and Psychotherapy* (New York: Rebman Company, [1899] 1907), pp. 126–133; and Moll, *Hypnotism*, pp. 129–130.

6. *JB*, p. 280 (my emphasis).

what follows: *"Those around her still saw nothing of this."*[7] Clearly, Breuer held to his diagnosis *in spite of* the Pappenheim family's incredulity, and perhaps even *in opposition to* the family's opinion in the matter.

The rest wasn't long in coming. "At the beginning of December she developed convergent strabismus. An eye specialist diagnosed paresis of the abducens, which I was convinced it was not. On 11 December the patient took to her bed, and did not leave it again until 1 April. A series of severe disorders developed in rapid succession, *apparently for the first time.*"[8]

---

7. *Ibid.* (my emphasis).
8. *Ibid.* (my emphasis).

CHAPTER EIGHT

Simulation

"Apparently for the first time"? Let's try a different hypothesis: that the onset of Bertha Pappenheim's strange "illness" coincided with Breuer's diagnosis of it. Her hysteria probably needed little else to set it in motion. All the indications are that Bertha was literally suffocated by her family atmosphere and sought to escape it by any means possible, including illness. But without the permission afforded by Breuer's diagnosis, her flight into illness very likely would have occurred at another time, and in a different form.

"Hysteria" is not a real illness, as we know, and its features vary according to the medical theory that frames it (in fact, "hysteria" is only one of many names for this sort of transport, or trance). Like so many other "neuroses," "mental illnesses," or "psychosomatic disorders," but more blatantly and spectacularly so, hysteria is an illness that exists for the sake of the cure. The symptoms claimed for it (and the trance states that normally make up their substratum) are distress signals, calls for help, cries for attention—which is to say, they are always requests for therapy and healing—so the symptoms closely match the diagnoses and theories of the doctors who respond to these appeals. What we usually call "suggestion" in hysteria is only an effect of that commonplace mimetism by which the patient produces all the symptoms the doctor is looking for (sometimes tossing in a few more for good measure), all the better to bequeath them to the doctor later on. To judge from the evidence, Bertha Pappenheim was a past master of this game: her symptoms were made to be cured, and as each one disappeared, she came up with another. In this sense, Breuer didn't so much uncover his patient's "hysteria" as unleash it, by showing her that he was ready to play the game called Hysteria. The first symptom of Bertha Pappenheim's hysteria was Breuer's diagnosis of it.

Obviously, this brings up the whole question of simulation, in hysteria generally and particularly in Bertha Pappenheim's treatment. Were all the episodes of paralysis, the muscle contractures, the anesthesia, the hallucinations, the aphasia, the "reminiscences" merely faked, simulated, by young Bertha Pappenheim so that she could meet Breuer's expectations? Ever since Charcot and Freud, we have grown so accustomed to regarding hysterical simulation as an outmoded, reactionary notion that we simply brush the thought off. The archhysteric of psychoanalysis faked her symptoms? What a ridiculous, indecent idea! And yet, as Swales and Schweighofer both point out,[1] this is exactly what Bertha Pappenheim herself said at the end of her treatment with Breuer. In the *Studies*, Breuer briefly alludes to this point: "At a time when, after the hysterical phenomena had ceased, the patient was passing through a temporary [!] depression, she brought up a number of childish fears and self-reproaches, and among them [was] the idea that she had not been ill at all and that the whole business had been simulated."[2] This account is corroborated (for once) by the Kreuzlingen documents. In his letter to Robert Binswanger of mid-June 1882 Breuer notes: "Today the patient is suffering from slight hysterical insanity, confessing at the moment to all kinds of deceptions, genuine or not."[3] Bertha apparently persisted in her declarations, for Breuer's preliminary report, submitted at the end of the same month, takes this issue up again: "Her present contention that her entire illness is an invention is quite certainly false, even if individual elements are not genuine."[4]

It's no accident, of course, that Breuer felt the need later on to speak of "catharsis" in connection with Bertha Pappenheim's treatment. Her illness was clearly a mimesis, a "private theater," a dramatic performance put on for her

---

1. Swales, "Freud, Breuer, and the Blessed Virgin," *passim*; Schweighofer, pp. 86 ff. and *passim*. Swales and Schweighofer both seem to have arrived independently at the thesis of Bertha's simulation, which makes the convergence of their analyses all the more remarkable. My only reservation is that they both see simulation too narrowly, in terms of fraud and lying; simulation is something more, and something else.
2. *SH*, p. 46.
3. *JB*, p. 293.
4. *Ibid.*, p. 295 (translation modified).

physician, and there are all sorts of indications that Breuer was fully aware of it. For example, when Bertha asked Breuer in Italian, some days after her father's death, "*E vero il mio padre è morto?*" (Is it true that my father is dead?), he told her that she knew very well he was.[5] And, referring to the patient's many suicide attempts during her stay at the Inzensdorf Sanatorium, Breuer describes them as "really quite harmless."[6] Breuer evidently wasn't taken in by his patient's "caprices" and "whims," so why did he refuse to believe her when she said she had taken him for a ride? Why did he insist so on her absolute "trustworthiness"?[7] Why did he write, "I am firmly convinced that the phenomena witnessed during this time [the winter of 1881] were perfectly genuine"?[8]

Looking more closely, we quickly see that Breuer's conviction has to do with the strictly *hypnotic* phenomena (protracted muscular spasms, paralyses, anesthesia, and so forth) that Bertha Pappenheim displayed, not with her "caprices." As Breuer explains in his preliminary report to Binswanger, he doesn't see how Bertha could have simulated "a contracture of the right arm lasting one-and-a-half years (and of the right leg lasting nine months) which would relax neither when she was asleep nor under intoxication with 5.00 chloral."[9] For a physiologist like Breuer, as for his colleagues Benedikt and Heidenhain, no

---

5. *Ibid.*, p. 284.
6. *Ibid.*, p. 286.
7. *Ibid.*, p. 277; *SH*, p. 43.
8. *JB*, p. 283.
9. *JB*, p. 283.

psychological cause could have explained such a physical performance. Something *real* had to be behind it—something physiological, inaccessible to the hysteric's conscious will. We find the same logic at work in Charcot and the Salpêtrière school: the conviction that the symptoms of hysteria are not simulated rests in turn on the conviction that the hypnotized subject is a "human machine."[10] Take, Charcot says, a hysterical subject in a deep cataleptic state, arm held out horizontally, and a subject who simulates this action. Now, using a Marey tambour, measure the oscillations of the two subjects' extended arms: the hysterical subject's arm won't move at all, but the simulating subject's will (see Figure 1).[11]

Finally, though, this positivist conviction, the source of so many illusions, must be punctured. The physical performance of subjects in hypnotic trance, amazing though it may be, is completely compatible with the idea of simulation as a voluntary, deliberate activity. Hypnotized subjects, even when they are cataleptic and anesthetized, are never just automatons at the mercy of the hypnotist's suggestions. Not only do subjects never lose consciousness, they also always "know all about" what they are pretending to shut out (the pain they are asked not to feel, the muscular fatigue they are asked to ignore, the objects they are asked not to see, the "selves" or

---

10. Charcot, writing about the cataleptic state of the hypnotized subject, says: "we see before us the *human machine* in all its simplicity, dreamt by de la Mettrie" (*Clinical Lectures on Diseases of the Nervous System*, vol. III, p. 290).

11. *Ibid.*, pp. 14–18.

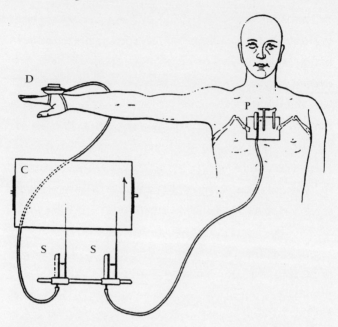

Figure 1—Diagram showing the arrangement of the apparatus in the experiments on cataleptic immobility. **D**, pressure drum of Marey; **P**, pneumograph; **C**, revolving cylinder; **S**, stylograph.

"personalities" from which they are asked to dissociate). Thus Ernest Hilgard, following in the footsteps of many other researchers, has demonstrated that even in the deepest hypnotic states there is always a "hidden observer" who is present at the spectacle of the trance. Hilgard quotes one of his own subjects: "When I'm in hypnosis, I'm imagining, letting myself pretend, but somewhere the hidden observer knows what's really going on."[12]

---

12. Ernest R. Hilgard, *Divided Consciousness: Multiple Controls in Human Thought and Action* (New York: Wiley-Interscience, [1977], 1986, 2nd edition), p. 209.

This is just what Bertha Pappenheim said, too, speaking of her "observer brain."[13] Breuer, citing Bertha's alternation between her normal state (or "real self") and her *condition seconde* (or hypnoid "bad self"), writes: "Nevertheless, though her two states were thus sharply separated, not only did the secondary state intrude into the first one, but—and this was at all events frequently true, and even when she was in a very bad condition—a clear-sighted and calm observer (*Beobachter*) sat, as she put it, in a corner of her brain and looked at all the mad business."[14] The mad business was show business: Bertha, playing her role (her second "personality") on the stage of hysteria, was also watching from the wings, as spectator of her own theatricality. The paradox of the trance (of hysteria) is nothing other than the "paradox of acting," as Diderot put it,[15] which is why Bertha concluded that "the whole business had been simulated."

Saying this may have been her way, at the time, of taking revenge on Breuer for his unwillingness to go on playing the game. But is that any reason to disbelieve what she said? In the *Studies*, Breuer invokes the notion of retrospective illusion: "Once a disorder of this kind has cleared up and the two states of consciousness have once more become merged into one, the patients, looking back at the

---

13. *JB*, p. 283: "It is true, however, as she herself often remarked, that even in her worst periods there was an 'observer brain' somewhere in her mind, observing with accuracy and acuteness, often giving her information about quite obscure matters."

14. *SH*, p. 46.

15. Denis Diderot, *The Paradox of Acting*/William Archer, *Masks or Faces* (New York: Hill and Wang, 1957).

past, see themselves as the single undivided personality which was aware of all the nonsense; they think they could have prevented it if they had wanted to, and thus they feel as though they had done all the mischief deliberately."[16] We can recognize this fallacious argument, also used today by American theorists of Multiple Personality Disorder: it is the argument for "dissociation of consciousness"—in other words, the argument for "the unconscious." The argument goes like this: Bertha, in personality A, was unconscious of what personality B was up to; therefore, she (personality A) was not simulating. Her hypnoid, unconscious "bad self," living the autonomous life of an automaton, was *really* separate from her normal, conscious self. When all is said and done, the hypothesis of the unconscious was (and is) simply an end run around the hypothesis of simulation, by way of arguing that the hysteric's right hand doesn't know (or forgets, or represses) what the left hand is doing.

Bertha Pappenheim thought otherwise. She knew very well that if her arm went into a contracture, it was because she had decided it would—*and that her decision did nothing to prevent the contracture from being real*. Simulation is not lying. It is the creation of a new reality. We can't play a role without *incarnating* it. How to play Lady Macbeth without adopting the actual movements of a sleepwalker? How to play Kleist's Penthesileia without actually alternating between two "personalities"? And how to imitate anesthesia without becoming *actually* insensitive to

---

16. *SH*, p. 46.

pain? Hysteria and hypnosis are not less real for being simulated. On the contrary, they are *surreal*[17] in the sense of simulation's being pushed to the point where the body goes along with it. How this happens is a mystery (the mystery known as "psychosomatics"), but the mystery in no way negates the fact that the process is a simulative one, and that simulation produces physical effects that are perfectly real. Fritz Schweighofer, with his zeal for de-mystification, accuses Bertha Pappenheim of having simulated hypnosis, by which he means that her paralysis and contractures were false, not real.[18] But this is only the mirror image of the mistake that Breuer makes when he claims that Bertha's spasms and paralysis *were* real (that is, not simulated). In reality (if we can call it that), simulation is always real—*surreal*—which is why it is so difficult for experimental psychologists to establish a criterion that would allow them to distinguish, with any certainty, a "true" hypnotized subject from a skillful simulator.[19] It's because, as Milton Erickson so neatly puts it, "*The best simulation is an actualization*":[20] the best way of simulating hypnosis is actually to fall into a hypnotic state.

---

17. Recall how the notion of "surreality" is introduced in Breton's *First Surrealist Manifesto*: "I believe in the future resolution of these two states, dream and reality, which are seemingly so contradictory, into a kind of absolute reality, or *surreality*, if one may so speak" (André Breton, *Manifestoes of Surrealism*, translated by Richard Seaver and Helen R. Lane [Ann Arbor: The University of Michigan Press, 1969], p. 14).

18. Schweighofer, *Das Privattheater der Anna O.*, pp. 96–97.

19. See Martin Orne's classic article, "The Nature of Hypnosis: Artifact and Essence," *The Journal of Abnormal and Social Psychology* 58 (1959), pp. 277–299.

20. Milton H. Erickson, *Advanced Techniques of Hypnosis and Therapy* (New York: Grune & Stratton, 1967), p. 129.

There's no doubt about it: Bertha Pappenheim was a gifted simulator. Her illness, like it or not, was as real (as surreal) as they get—until the day she decided that this sterile and desperate game was no longer worth the trouble. And yet her illness had no other reality (no other surreality) than this: it was a childish game she played with a rather gullible Viennese doctor, a game whose strange rules the two of them made up together as they went along. The game goes on.

What Did Freud Tell Marie Bonaparte?

Whoever proposes to research the history of psycho-analysis should understand that he or she is about to enter a strange universe, one ruled by secrecy, rumor, and the manipulation of information. I could give many examples but will limit myself here to a single one.

On November 12, 1985, the *New York Times*, with much fanfare, announced the forthcoming publication of the "journals" (note the plural) of Princess Marie Bonaparte, under the editorship of New York psychoanalyst Frank Hartman. Daniel Goleman, a correspondent for the *Times*, wrote in his article that Marie Bonaparte's daughter, Princess Eugénie of Greece, had given Dr. Hartman permission to publish them. Goleman added that the publication of these "journals," long withheld from the public eye (notwithstanding their having been put at Ernest Jones's disposal while he was working on his biography of Sigmund Freud), could "result in [the] rewriting

[of] portions of psychoanalytic history."[1] Quoting Dr. Hartman, Goleman included bits and pieces of Marie Bonaparte's journal and, among other "scoops," offered this one: "Freud told the Princess that one of the reasons Josef Breuer, his first collaborator, stopped treating his famous patient Anna O. was that Breuer had become so infatuated with his patient that his wife, out of jealousy, attempted suicide—a fact never before brought to light. Most sources give Breuer's panic over Anna O.'s hysteric pregnancy as a main reason for his halting the treatment."[2]

More than a decade later, this much anticipated publication still hasn't seen the light of day. For the present volume, I wanted to quote the passage from Marie Bonaparte's journal that allegedly deals with Mathilde Breuer's suicide attempt. Anxious to check my sources, I phoned Dr. Hartman, who readily confirmed that this episode is mentioned in the journal.[3] But he declined to provide me with a copy of the passage, or to give me any information at all about the date of the entry, its exact nature, and the provenance of the document in his possession.

Was Dr. Hartman simply exercising his most basic right? I don't think so. It's one thing to withhold a document in order to maintain medical confidentiality or

---

1. Daniel Goleman, "Freud's Mind: New Details Revealed in Documents," *New York Times*, November 12, 1985, p. C1.
2. *Ibid.*, p. C5.
3. Telephone conversation of December 30, 1994, followed by two more conversations, in March and May of 1995.

protect people's privacy; it's quite another to keep it to oneself after trumpeting its existence in the press. Historians who make public use of the documents in their possession are morally obligated to allow other researchers access to those documents. The failure to do so is an appropriation of historical truth.

I don't know what rights Dr. Hartman has to Marie Bonaparte's journal(s), just as, more generally, I don't know why documents that were generously made available to Ernest Jones continue to be withheld from other historians.[4] What I do know is that historians who exercise complete monopoly over archives and information (as so often happens in Freud studies) can write what they like with impunity. As long as Freud's legitimate and bastard heirs share their documents only with other true believers, the history of psychoanalysis will remain susceptible to every kind of manipulation—and will continue to attract a highly justified suspicion. It's entirely too easy to accuse "revisionist" historians of paranoia and interpretive delirium when documents that could set the record straight are systematically kept under lock and key.

Puzzled by Dr. Hartman's attitude, I attempted to put myself in touch with several people whom I thought might be able to confirm or deny what Dr. Hartman had told the *Times*. Mrs. Tatiana Fruchaud, Marie Bonaparte's granddaughter and legal owner of her archives, evidently

---

4. The original of Marie Bonaparte's journal (singular) is at the Library of Congress, in Washington, D.C., where access to it is totally restricted.

saw no advantage in responding to the letter I sent her. Daniel Goleman, by contrast, willingly confirmed that Dr. Hartman had shown him a document (written in English) that supposedly was a reproduction of Marie Bonaparte's journal. Goleman couldn't vouch for this document's authenticity, however, nor was he able to recall whether he had actually read the passage on Mathilde Breuer's suicide attempt or simply repeated in his article what Dr. Hartman had told him.[5]

Peter Swales, whom I knew had been in contact with Dr. Hartman in the past, was extremely helpful, as always. About fifteen years ago, he told me, Dr. Hartman had quoted several anecdotes to him from Marie Bonaparte's journal; Swales was able to corroborate most of them later, in the course of his own research. He also told me about a dinner at Dr. Hartman's, where the psychoanalyst brought up the subject of Marie Bonaparte's journal and Swales himself had the chance to skim through a typescript written in English. Upon returning home, Swales made some notes from memory on what he had read. When I told him about Dr. Hartman's reaction to my request for information, Peter Swales kindly gave me permission to reproduce the following passage from his notes. The passage directly concerns Breuer and Anna O. (and represents, he says, about 10 to 15 percent of the notes manuscript). But he stresses his inability to guarantee the absolute reliability of these hastily written notes. I have bracketed his interpolations,

---

5. Telephone conversation, May 17, 1995.

as well as the introductory paragraph describing the circumstances in which the notes were made:

[13 December 1981.

Last night had dinner at Frank Hartman's with Harold Blum[6] and his wife, Else. During dinner Hartman began telling snippets from his Marie Bonaparte material on Freud—e.g., that Freud didn't have his three sons circumcised. Then he took out a typescript manuscript of either the so-called Summary or the Journal—I am almost sure it was the Summary. I took two or three looks at it during the others' conversation, flicking through the pages rapidly with my eyes focused on the one page or other that interested me. Thus I got to spend four or five minutes, all in all, imprinting what I saw on my mind. As I sit here, I can see certain information sufficiently clearly that the following can be relied upon for accuracy at least 95 percent, probably 100 percent (i.e., I am not writing down stuff I cannot recall properly].

[. . .]

[Breuer and Anna O. are discussed twice in the manuscript—here I condense the two discussions.]

Confronted by Breuer's almost obsessional discussing of Anna O. all the time, his wife Mathilde made a suicide attempt. Breuer broke off the treatment. But the same night he was called back and Anna confessed to him that she was pregnant by him.[7]

Breuer was a vain man, believing himself to be quite "irresistible," so he automatically attributed this to himself—whereas on hearing about it, as Freud claimed, he himself saw it as a phenomenon of the neurosis itself.

---

6. Successor to Dr. Kurt Eissler as head of the Sigmund Freud Archives, Inc.

7. Peter Swales assures me that he was quite aware of the oddness of this last formulation at the time he wrote it down.

Remembering Anna O.

Freud said the real reason he broke with Breuer was over his misrepresentation of what really had happened in publishing the case of Anna O. in 1895. Freud quoted the line about Anna's mental equilibrium[8] [maybe he corrupted it in doing so??] and declared that Anna O. was not in fact cured but remained ill for some time after. Freud said Breuer was a man of far superior intellect to himself; but he was one who had no "moral courage"—a virtue Freud attributed to himself in saying this is where he scored, as opposed to Breuer. He was ready to face opposition, Breuer was not.

After Freud had in 1914 [On the History of the Psycho-Analytic Movement] *published a more suggestive account of what really happened, Breuer's daughter asked her father about it; and one day Breuer came to see Freud, saying: "What have you done to me!"*

Freud said he did not himself know Anna O., though his wife had done so before the marriage. Anna O. was "from Frankfurt," says the manuscript. With glee, Freud told Marie Bonaparte what Anna O. was now doing—running a girls' home and campaigning against prostitution—all a preoccupation with sexuality!

These notes, interesting as they are, cannot by themselves prove the reliability of the document obtained by Dr. Hartman. Moreover, as Swales points out, the nature of the document itself is unclear. Is it a transcription and translation of Marie Bonaparte's original journal (or of excerpts from it)? Is it the "summary" sent to Jones? Elisabeth Roudinesco, I knew, had access to the original

---

8. *SH*, pp. 40–41: "After this she left Vienna and travelled for a while; but it was a considerable time before she regained her mental balance entirely. Since then she has enjoyed complete health."

manuscript of Marie Bonaparte's journal, and I asked her to check and see whether it actually did contain a passage about a suicide attempt by Mathilde Breuer. I gave her an approximate date (1925 or a bit later) on the basis of information that Swales had provided.

Marie Bonaparte's journal is an impressive thicket of barely legible notes, scrawled in a telegraphic style and in many languages, and as such is not easy to consult (I can vouch for that, having once had the opportunity to glance through it). Nevertheless, Roudinesco managed to locate an enigmatic entry on Breuer and Anna O. dated October 17, 1925: "Breuer and Fräulein Anna O. Confession 10 years later" [?]. Roudinesco also consulted Célia Bertin, Marie Bonaparte's biographer,[9] who said that Marie Bonaparte had nowhere mentioned any suicide attempt by Mathilde Breuer. Therefore, Roudinesco concluded that the document in Dr. Hartman's possession was a forgery concocted out of thin air, and that Peter Swales's notes on it were definitely not to be trusted. It now appeared that there was nothing to the whole affair, and that my own suspicions about the story Freud had told Marie Bonaparte were also unfounded.

Not long afterward, as luck would have it, Roudinesco was consulting Marie Bonaparte's journal again, this time for completely different reasons, and stumbled across the very passage whose existence had seemed to her so doubtful. I reproduce it here with Elisabeth

---

9. Célia Bertin, *Marie Bonaparte: A Life* (New York: Harcourt Brace Jovanovich, 1982).

Roudinesco's kind permission, and with my thanks for her generous help in this research. My interpolations, as well as my translations from the German, are bracketed in the passage that follows:

Freud's memories as reported by him during these three months of analysis.
[. . .]

The 16th of December [1927], in Vienna, Freud told me the Breuer story. His wife tried to kill herself towards the end of Anna = Bertha's treatment. The rest is well known: Anna's relapse, her fantasy of pregnancy, Breuer's flight.

Breuer's daughter questioned her father about it. He confessed everything that Freud had written in the Selbstdarstellung.

Br[euer] a[n] Freud: Was haben *Sie* mir ja angestellt! *[Breuer to Freud: What have you got me into!]*
[. . .]

Fr. "Wenn Sie Breuer gekannt hätten, der war geistig [,] mir geistig viel überlegener. Nur eines habe ich gehabt: der Mut, gegen die Majorität allein zu stehen, der Glaube an mich selbst. . . ." Breuer klagelich: "Man ist immer weniger vereinsamt als man glaubt" *[Freud: "If you had known Breuer, he was a great mind, a mind quite superior to me. I had only one thing: courage to stand up against the majority, faith in myself. . . ." Breuer, plaintively: "We are always less alone than we would like to believe."']*

Notice that this document partly confirms the notes that Swales took, since it mentions not only Mathilde Breuer's suicide attempt but also the moral courage that Freud appears to have attributed so generously to himself (a piece of personal information shared with Marie Bonaparte but not reported in the *Times* article). Another memory of Freud, which appears on the copied page of Marie Bonaparte's journal that Elisabeth Roudinesco sent me, is also found in Swales's notes: Freud told the Princess that, with one exception, he had never kissed the hand of any woman, the exception being his friend Fleischl-Marxow's mother, when she was at her son's deathbed. But Swales's notes also mention other personal confidences that Freud shared with Marie Bonaparte, which are not found in the passage turned up by Elisabeth Roudinesco. The discrepancy between the two documents is easily explained, however, if we remember that Swales's notes say he condensed passages from two different places in Dr. Hartman's typescript—passages that also, we may suppose, came from two different places in the original manuscript of the journal. It is therefore to be hoped that Elisabeth Roudinesco will soon find the corresponding passages in Marie Bonaparte's original journal, so that the two versions can be compared.

But the differences in wording between the two documents[10] can be explained in other ways as well. Indeed, it is entirely possible that the document in Dr. Hartman's keeping (the basis for Peter Swales's notes) differs greatly from the original manuscript copy of the journal in Elisabeth Roudinesco's possession. In a letter to Ernest Jones

---

10. The most important of these differences has to do with the date of the "confession" that Breuer made to his daughter Dora: after the publication of *An Autobiographical Study* (the *Selbstdarstellung*, in 1925), or after the publication of *On the History of the Psychoanalytic Movement* (1914)?

dated June 18, 1954 (a letter deposited with the Institute of Psycho-Analysis in London), Marie Bonaparte, writing in English, announces that she has sent Jones a large "selection" of notes on her journal, which are likely to be of interest to him. The letter is reproduced here with my thanks to Pearl King, honorary archivist of the Institute, for permitting access to this document, to which access is ordinarily restricted. Again, my interpolations are bracketed:

In the South,[11] *I worked for you. Extracted from my notes written during my analysis what might be of interest for you. No doubt more than you will probably need. But it was better to give you everything together.*

There are a few [illegible] *lines* [?] *about the past* [?].

Different views of Freud on diverse topics.

I also found the words we exchanged about Mounet Sully in Oedipus Rex. *He did not see him in that play, unfortunately (see p. 52 of my manuscript).*

I hope you can read my writing—I had no time to have it typed.

Excuse the mistakes I may have made in German!

Let's suppose, as we can without too great a stretch of the imagination, that while Marie Bonaparte was assembling her notes for Jones, she not only made them more legible but also put them in order, adding all sorts of missing links not found in her private journal. If so, and if this is the "summary" in Dr. Hartman's possession, then

---

11. Her residence at Saint-Tropez, where Jones and his wife had just been for an extended visit (and where, we can imagine, all sorts of Freud anecdotes must have been exchanged).

Swales's notes, far from being less reliable than Marie Bonaparte's original journal, are actually based on a version that is more developed—and thus much more interesting—than the original.

But these are only hypotheses that cannot be corroborated for the time being. Dr. Hartman could easily clarify these points but refuses to do so. Moreover, the manuscript that Marie Bonaparte sent to Jones in 1954 is no longer to be found in the Jones Archives of the Institute of Psycho-Analysis in London. These archives now contain only a variety of notes that Marie Bonaparte sent to Ernest Jones in the early 1950s; there is no manuscript of the length (at least fifty-two pages) that she refers to in the letter I cite here. Paul Roazen was able to consult all the Jones papers before access to them was restricted, and he assures me that this manuscript had already vanished from the archives by the 1960s.

Where is it now? Who slipped it out of the Institute's archives? Openness not being the strong suit of psychoanalytic institutions, we certainly cannot expect to have this little mystery solved anytime soon. Nor are we soon likely to discover just what Freud really did say to his friend Princess Marie Bonaparte as she lay on his analytic couch.

A Letter from Hanna Breuer to Ernest Jones

*T*he following letter was sent to Ernest Jones by Breuer's daughter-in-law, Hanna Breuer, shortly after the publication (1953) of the first volume of Jones's biography of Freud. The letter deals only indirectly with Bertha Pappenheim's treatment, but its inclusion seems fitting here, since the letter shows something of the discrepancy between Freud's presentation of his relationship with his old friend and Breuer's relatives' description of it. Between the lines, we can also discern the silence that was Breuer's response to Freud's public insinuations.

The existence of this letter, whose original can be found at the Institute of Psycho-Analysis in London, was first revealed by Paul Roazen, who (as mentioned in Appendix I) had the opportunity to read the Jones papers before access to them was restricted.[1] The letter cited here is taken from a typescript copy in the Ellenberger Archives in Paris, where it can be freely consulted by anyone with an interest in it. I thank Sonu

---

1. Paul Roazen, *Freud and His Followers* (New York: Knopf, 1975), pp. 80 and 558, 24n.

Shamdasani for finding this document and bringing it to my attention. My thanks are due also to Mrs. Marie Kann for her kind permission to reprint this letter of her mother's.

Hanna Breuer
112 Haven Ave.
New York 32, N.Y.   April 21, 1954

Dear Dr. Jones:

My sister-in-law Käthy Breuer in London told me in a recent letter that Ilse Hellman has been in touch with you about the error concerning Dora Breuer,[2] and that you were quite willing to accept corrections before the imminent issue of a second edition of your book. This gives me courage to write to you, although what I have to say is not a correction in the strict sense.

Coming from someone so closely connected with Josef Breuer, my remarks may not carry conviction with you, and this is why I hesitated. However, I want to try.

It is a pity you have not known Josef Breuer personally. If you had, his motives in acting as he did, on certain occasions, would have been as plain to you as they are to

---

2. An allusion to Freud's story about Dora Breuer's supposed conception in Venice, after the precipitate interruption of Anna O.'s treatment (see p. 24).

me and, indeed, to anyone who did know him. This refers to your comments on pages 145, 255 and 256.[3]

May I comment on two points:

1) You seem to assume with Freud that Breuer had some tendency to keep his younger friend under a

---

3. The passages which Hanna Breuer refers to are the following: 1. "One evening at the Breuers' Freud spoke of his approaching marriage, but when Mathilde Breuer entered into the theme with interest, Breuer started up crying, 'For God's sake, don't egg him on to get married,' and he advised Freud not to think of it for another two years [letter to Martha Bernays of April 18, 1886]. It was the first sign of some change in Breuer's attitude toward Freud, one that proved fateful to their friendship in years to come. His former encouragement was being replaced by an attitude of dampening any enthusiasm of Freud's, both in his personal life and his later work in psychopathology. His attitude had been most satisfactory so long as Freud was a young son in need of help, but he seemed to grudge his growing independence, as many fathers do with their children. However, it was some years yet before this change became evident" (Jones, *The Life and Work of Sigmund Freud*, 1, p. 145). 2. Having cited Freud's "strong words" about Breuer after their break, Jones goes on to write: "They go much beyond the actual complaints Freud formulates. Breuer, so it would appear, had certain characteristics which were particularly antipathetic to Freud's nature. One was a weakness in his personality that made it hard for him ever to take a definite stand on any question. The other was a pettifogging kind of censoriousness which would induce him to mar any appreciation or praise by searching out a small point open to criticism—an attitude very alien to Freud's openhearted and generous spirit" (*ibid.*, p. 255). 3. "It is plain that Freud now resented the burden of the old debt of gratitude he owed Breuer, one that could in part be estimated in the concrete terms of money. Early in 1898 he made the first attempt to repay an installment of this. Breuer, who was probably loath to accept what he must long have regarded as a gift, wanted to set off against it an amount he considered Freud should be paid for medical attention on a relative of his. Freud seems to have interpreted this as an endeavor to retain the old tutelage, and bitterly resented Breuer's response. [...] And in all this sad story one has to remember Freud's confessed need for periodic experience of intense love and hate, one which his self-analysis had not yet softened" (*ibid.*, pp. 255–256).

kind of fatherly control; that he "seemed to grudge his growing independence" and

2) you seem to take at face value Freud's complaint about Breuer's being given to "a pettifogging kind of censoriousness," and discouraging him by his criticisms.

My comment is this: I have known Josef Breuer not only as long as I lived, which does not mean much; but I have known him about 25 years of my adult life. As a member of the family, I would have inevitably noticed at some time or other, a tendency in him to dominate, if there had been one. But the opposite was true. There was not a trace of it in him. Just to quote one example: my husband told me that his father had sent him away to continue his studies abroad in order to facilitate transition to adult independence. And never, never had there been the slightest attempt to interfere with our several young menages. It is difficult to say adequately how much it meant to my husband to have his father around until he, himself, was well over fifty. A tendency as the one you suggest would imply some ever so slight disposition to self-importance or vanity. Well, this was simply lacking in my father-in-law—it simply was non-existent.

The explanation for Josef Breuer's strong resistance to Freud's marriage (p. 145) to me, is simple and natural. He was afraid of what married life without sufficient financial basis would do to Freud; and when, years later, he thought of a way to prevent Freud from paying his "debt,"

Freud could have known better than to interpret the suggestion as "an endeavor to retain his old Tutelage."

You contend that there must have been some basis to Freud's complaints about petty criticisms, as contrasted with his own openhearted and generous spirits. Well, I have never known a person more given to happy and often enthusiastic recognition of others' merits.

On p. 242, you quote Breuer as writing to Fliess about Freud's intellect "soaring at its highest" and comparing himself to the hen that gazes at the hawk.[4] This remark is most typical of Breuer. May I go on from there to the conclusion that his friendship for the younger man was long past the stage of sympathetic encouragement. In proportion to his growing admiration, his honest friendship *had to* become exacting and critical, because, for the mature Freud's work, in Breuer's judgment, nothing short of perfection could be tolerated. So he may well have wanted to eliminate any, even minor flaws. To me this is very obvious and very different from [a] "pettifogging kind of censoriousness." It is wholly in line with Breuer's way of thinking. (He certainly applied it to his own papers.) Unfortunately, it seems, Freud could not, or would not, take it.

Your summing up on page 256 ("and in all that sad story one has to remember Freud's confessed need . . .")

---

4. *Ibid.*, p. 242: "Freud's intellect is soaring at its highest. I gaze after him as a hen at a hawk."

makes me hope that my interpretations may find at least some partial acceptance with you. There is one person within your reach who could confirm my views. However, being just another daughter-in-law she may not be considered a more unbiased witness than I. I am referring to Käthy Breuer.

May I mention that I have never heard a word from my father-in-law concerning his relationship to Freud. True, when I became a member of the family in 1906 it had long been a thing of the past. But how deeply the break must have wounded Breuer can be guessed from a significant little incident that happened when he was already an old man: he walked in the street (in Vienna) when, suddenly, he saw Freud coming head on towards him. Instinctively, he opened his arms. Freud passed professing not to see him.

Your fascinating book will be read by millions of people and by future generations. I am most anxious that the fine and truthful picture of an unusually good man, that of Josef Breuer, as it emerges from those pages, should not suffer through what I think are minor inaccuracies.

Forgive me for putting everything before you so squarely and uncompromisingly.

Very sincerely yours,
Hanna Breuer

Catalepsy and Mesmerism
Moriz Benedikt

*T*he article that follows is the account of a lecture delivered by
Moriz Benedikt to the Viennese Society of Physicians on March
3, 1880, in the wake of the scandal created by the hypnotist Carl
Hansen's performances at Vienna's Ringtheater. Unlike the original
text of the lecture, later revised and published in Benedikt's book Hypnotismus und Suggestion *(1894), this text, published in the*
Wiener medizinische Blätter *(10, 1880, pp. 250–252), is not
from Benedikt's own hand. Nevertheless, I decided to use it here because
Benedikt's published text, by comparison with the lecture originally presented to the Society of Physicians, seems to have undergone considerable revision. I hope above all to show this lecture's potential impact on
Breuer (and, by extension, on Bertha Pappenheim), and so I have cho-
sen to reproduce what appears to be the version of this text that is closest
to the lecture given in March 1880. (Henri Ellenberger, in The Discovery of the Unconscious, *refers to another account, which appeared in the* Wiener klinische Wochenschrift, *and which I
have not been able to locate at the indicated date.)*

Credit for calling attention to this account's existence—and, more generally, for underlining the role that this lecture must have played in Bertha Pappenheim's treatment—must go to Uffe Hansen.

"The matter which currently grips doctors and laymen alike has proven once again the necessity of applying to medicine the strict principles of the critique of pure reason and ethics." Thus began Dr. Benedikt's lecture.

Experiments with cataleptics[1] *are experiments on living people.* The ethical and mental reliability of the experiment's subjects comes into consideration, and indeed the level of mental reliability is particularly low in catalepsy, because consciousness is very deceptive in relation to inner processes. Moreover, the experimental conditions are far less favorable than they are with animal experiments.

What holds for the experimental subjects also holds for the experimenter, particularly if he is pursuing extramedical motives; but even ethically sound experts can stray far from the truth in their opinions and presentation.

A further source of error is the type of reception by one's peers in science. Outside of the courtroom, judgment does not simply follow upon examination, nor does condemnation simply follow proof of guilt.

All truths which have emerged in the history of science, and which did not immediately receive the

---

1. Hypnotized persons: Benedikt, in this text, systematically uses the words *catalepsy, cataleptics,* and so on, in place of *hypnosis* and related words.

stamp of approval from the intellectual establishment, have produced, on the one hand, a powerful group of Pharisees and, on the other, a more or less eccentric sect of adherents.

The lack of theoretical clarity in the original mesmeric procedures should not be deemed scandalous; otherwise, following that logic, doctors wouldn't be allowed to use any plant-derived substances, on the grounds that we don't thoroughly understand the mechanics of their effects—but then logic was never the strong suit of impassioned enemies.

The real scandal[2] is caused by the effects of mesmeric procedures, namely the cataleptic and cataleptiform manifestations. The doctors in Mesmer's time were appalled by the mysticism of these manifestations, and even though advances in brain physiology and in psychophysical thought have long since made possible the subsumption of cataleptic symptoms under the laws of nature, traditional prejudice and the sweet habit of casting aspersions on one's colleagues continue to hold sway.

The lecturer reports that he has often psychophysically analyzed the symptoms of catalepsy, particularly symptoms of the pathological and not the artificially induced catalepsy, and he intends to analyze them on a broader scale in his lecture. He emphasizes that the automatic movements are explained by experiments on animals whose brain hemispheres had been removed.

---

2. An allusion to the polemics and trial provoked by Carl Hansen's exhibitions.

Moreover, he has frequently come across the fact that cataleptics will perfectly reproduce, verbatim, a long series of acoustic impressions in foreign languages, impressions which they have passively absorbed years before. He explains that the brain takes in all impressions completely, down to the last detail, and this is so even for impressions one has paid little attention to. Under the right circumstances these impressions can cross the latency threshold, and can be transferred, with or without conscious intervention, to the articulation centers.

Just so, the brain is a photographic plate, which takes in all visual impressions, and under the proper conditions all the details, in their natural lighting and colors, can come into consciousness. This is the case with all other sense perceptions.

These vivid memories are frequent among cataleptics; the memories are externally projected in accordance with a physiological law, and they are completely real for the patients. This explains the patients' astonishing knowledge, and it partly explains their ability to see and hear over vast distances. A perception by means of one sense suffices to fully awaken the hallucinatory memory-image, which originally arose from different sense perceptions. Thus arise the phenomena of the so-called *transposition of the senses*; these phenomena are all the more marked when a single sense has become unusually acute.

Here the lecturer turns to the miraculous medical achievements of cataleptics. A photographic memory-image of a pharmacy appears before the cataleptic; he knows the content and the order of a series of jars, and he glibly combines this knowledge with a layman's knowledge of diseases—the chief miracle here is that even mesmeric doctors impute diagnostic and therapeutic miracles to the clairvoyant, while their opponents are foolish enough to contest rather than to accept these simple, bare facts. Far more valuable is the testimony of clairvoyants concerning their own conditions; in a clairvoyant state they possess hyperesthesia of the inner organs, which gives them the possibility of indicating the source from which their sickness stems.

The much admired prophecies of the clairvoyants rest in part on the simple drawing of conclusions, just as we can in general foresee events arising out of familiar, cyclic experiences. And in part their prophecies rest on the law by which even the little book of dreams is sometimes right, and the rest is a matter of faith for the faithful.

The uncanniness of the apparent higher development of the clairvoyants' individual powers has seduced their observers into regarding the clairvoyants' mental activity as superior. On the contrary, their mental activity is inferior in comparison with the normal state of mind. The clairvoyants give us cause to admire the genius of nature's ordinary powers.

Aside from the fact that as yet no clairvoyant has produced a worthy intellectual, artistic, or technical achievement, the very vividness of their memory-images prevents them from discerning between external and internal events, and from distinguishing the essential from the inessential. Were we not able to suppress countless impressions beneath the threshold of consciousness, we could not form any concepts, nor concentrate our attention, nor think or create.

The moral ecstasy has also been overestimated. When, through pathological suppression of the temptation toward vice, virtue comes to the fore, this has no ethical value for the individual, and the mute ecstasy is nothing other than the overwhelming expression of a somewhat transcendentally colored sensuality. Bernini has brilliantly captured this in his famed statue of Saint Teresa.

For one who knows how to think psychophysically, there is nothing mystical about clinical catalepsy; the same is true of artificial catalepsy. Artificial catalepsy has been produced through various means, to which the lecturer gives the collective name of "Cataleptica." These include such stimuli as sound, light, warmth, as well as metallic magnets, the fatigue due to staring at an object, the properly mesmeric procedures themselves (Hansen has thoroughly convinced the lecturer of their efficacy), and doubtless the imagination as well.

The lecturer remarks in passing that the properly mesmeric procedures cannot be seen as heat radiation, as Berger[3] claims, nor can they be seen as a means of exciting the imagination, as claimed long ago in the report by the French Academy of Sciences.[4] Until now, the majority of doctors and clinicians have regarded all the

---

3. O. Berger, a neurologist from Breslau who, like his colleague Heidenhain, developed an interest in Carl Hansen's exhibitions during Hansen's stay in their city.

4. An allusion to the conclusions of the royal commission set up by Louis XVI in 1784 to investigate Mesmer's "animal magnetism."

phenomena of artificial catalepsy as effects of imagination and simulation. The lecturer felt it was important to focus on this completely untenable hypothesis, in order to show how unscientific the clinical mind can be when confronted by a new question. Doubtless the imagination and the will can call forth cataleptic states; still, it makes no sense to suppose that a serving girl who wants to simulate catalepsy can recite long Bible passages in their original language, copy foreign writing with exactitude and speed, or give the position and contents of all the jars in a pharmacy, solely as a result of her willed simulation.

The experts thereby turn the achievements of the fakers into true miracles, and in comparison with these experts who are constantly talking about "exact science," the most dogged mesmerists' fools are colossal rationalists. Earlier, one got past such nonsense by a unanimous denial of the facts; today, this would be a pharisaical lie. The imagination and the will merely act as psychotoxic stimulants, which stimulate or exhaust the various brain centers; scientific logic commands us to study the objective laws of the effects of stimulation.

The lecturer dismantles the claim of the mesmerists that it is their *will* which influences the experimental subject, a critique that is all the more necessary since even Schopenhauer took this claim at face value and metaphysically exploited it.[5] The will plays a merely indirect role in that it serves to set the experimenter's muscles in a

---

5. An allusion to Schopenhauer's "Essay on Visions," in *Parerga and Paralipomena: Short Philosophical Essays* (Oxford: Clarendon Press, 1974).

state of strong tension, which seems to be necessary to the success of such experiments.

Regarding the danger of experiments in cataleptizing, this danger is unproven and is solely a product of theoretical speculation; such cataleptizing experiments have been performed on many, many people without harming them. Given that the experiments can always be broken off at once, imminent danger is a priori highly unlikely. The danger of a temporary spinal irritation can easily be avoided, and conversely, in many cases there is no better means for combating a case of spinal irritation than certain cataleptizing procedures. For the masses, the dangers are more of a mental and ethical nature in that great minds can be led astray by mesmeric experiments, and above all, doctors can be ethically led astray. In any case, first there should be a complete methodological clarification.

Finally, the lecturer urges the doctors and clinicians to test and to evaluate questions that arise more conscientiously, lest a layman should again have to supply the impetus to lead the scientific truth to triumph.

Translated by Diana George

Index